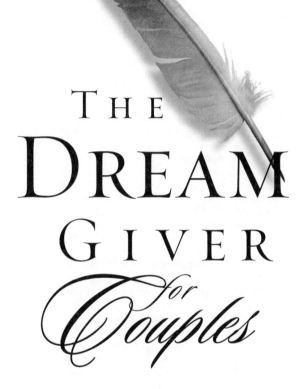

THE
DREAM
GIVER
for Couples

BRUCE & DARLENE MARIE
WILKINSON

Multnomah® Publishers *Sisters, Oregon*

The Dream Giver for Couples
published by Multnomah Publishers, Inc.
Based on *The Dream Giver* by Bruce Wilkinson
and David and Heather Kopp.

© 2004 by Exponential, Inc.
International Standard Book Number: 1-59052-460-8

Published in South Africa by Lux Verbi.BM

Unless otherwise indicated, Scripture quotations are from:
The Holy Bible, New King James Version © 1984 by Thomas Nelson, Inc.
Other Scripture quotations are from:
The Amplified Bible (AMP) © 1965, 1987 by Zondervan Publishing House.
The Amplified New Testament © 1958, 1987 by the Lockman Foundation.

Multnomah is a trademark of Multnomah Publishers, Inc.,
and is registered in the U.S. Patent and Trademark Office.
The colophon is a trademark of Multnomah Publishers, Inc.

Printed in the United States of America

For information:
MULTNOMAH PUBLISHERS, INC. · P. O. BOX 1720 · SISTERS, OR 97759

Library of Congress Cataloging-in-Publication Data

Wilkinson, Bruce.
    The dream giver for couples : living the marriage of your dreams / Bruce Wilkinson and Darlene Marie Wilkinson ; with Andres Cilliers.
        p. cm.
    ISBN 1-59052-460-8
    1. Spouses—Religious life. 2. Marriage—Religious aspects—Christianity. I. Wilkinson, Darlene. II. Cilliers, Andres. III. Wilkinson, Bruce Dream giver. IV. Title.
    BV4596.M3W53 2004
    248.8′44—dc22

                                                              2004015521

04 05 06 07 08 09—10 9 8 7 6 5 4 3 2 1 0

This book is for every couple
who has ever hoped or believed it is possible
to live the marriage of their dreams.

❦

Our deepest appreciation
to the incredible team at Multnomah Publishers,
to Rod Morris for his editorial assistance,
and to Andries Cilliers for his contribution to the parable;
to all our wonderful family and friends
who asked the Dream Giver
to bless this book;
and to the Dream Giver Himself,
who teaches us how to live
the marriage of our dreams.

Contents

PREFACE

$\mathcal{A}$re you living the marriage of your dreams? Imagine being asked that question instead of, "How long have you been married?" Couples around the world know there are two parts to the answer to that question: "We have been married for five years, and happily married for two." Wherever we go, we discover that many couples have lost the dream they started out with for their marriage.

That's why we'd like to share some principles we've learned that have the potential to change your marriage forever.

The Dream Giver for Couples is made up of two parts. Part One is a modern-day parable about Ordinary. In the original book, *The Dream Giver,* Ordinary was a Nobody who became a Somebody. He left his Comfort Zone in search of his Big Dream, which he discovered in the Land of Promise. That's where we pick up the story and continue it as the Dream Giver provides a wife for Ordinary and they set out on their next Big Dream together.

Part Two is designed to inspire you on your own journey as a married couple. Few things in life are more important to you and your spouse than your marriage relationship. Yet most things in life seem to become more important than the marriage of your dreams.

We had just ended a seminar on marriage when a very attractive couple approached us and confessed, "We both wanted a divorce but decided to attend your seminar before seeing a lawyer." They went on to share that after ten years of struggle, they had decided to give up. Then with tears in their eyes they said, "After hearing you teach on the roles of the wife and husband from God's perspective, we have asked each other's forgiveness and are returning home to start doing things God's way." That husband and wife are now back on the path to pursuing the marriage of their dreams.

If you've ever felt like the path to your dream marriage has led you into a wilderness, then take courage. Dream marriages take time. Dream marriages take commitment. Dream marriages take at least one person who will continue to fan the flame that may be threatening to go out.

It doesn't matter if you've been married one year or fifty. You may even be on the brink of stepping into, or

out of, this adventure called marriage. Regardless of
where you are today, the journey you are about to take
will give you new hope as you discover seven principles on
how to live the marriage of your dreams.

Affectionately,

Bruce and Darlene Marie

Johannesburg, South Africa

PART I

THE PARABLE
OF
ORDINARY

LIVING IN THE
LAND OF PROMISE

*N*ot very long ago and not so far away, Ordinary, a
Nobody from the Land of Familiar, set out to follow his
Big Dream. After an incredible journey, he made it to the
Land of Promise.

Finally, Ordinary thought to himself, *my Big Dream is a
reality!* It was true. The Dream Giver had faithfully
brought Ordinary to the City of Anybodies where great
needs existed. He was now a Somebody, making a
difference for the Dream Giver. The sheepish Anybodies,
whom he'd grown to love, were now walking upright and
looking at the world through shining eyes. Many of them
were even ready to pursue their own Big Dream.

Then, one day, something totally unexpected happened to Ordinary.

While planting Never-Ending Gardens with a group of Anybodies, he thought he heard the Dream Giver say, *Let me show you more.*

"More?" questioned Ordinary.

He quickly made his way to the city gate and looked toward the horizon. He saw the many more Lands of Promise waiting for him to claim for the Dream Giver. "My Big Dream in the City of Anybodies is nearly done," Ordinary said. "It is time for me to move on. The Dream Giver has a bright, new Dream awaiting me."

Ordinary knew that he must not simply choose his own course. So he waited for a sign from the Dream Giver as to his new direction. He waited and waited until he could scarcely wait any longer. In great anticipation, he walked to the edge of the city, opened the gate, and stepped outside.

"Oh," said Ordinary, "this feels strangely. . .uncomfortable."

As he turned to go back inside the city walls, he heard the Dream Giver's voice say, *One more thing is needed, and then you can go.*

One more thing? Ordinary wondered. What could it be? What did the Dream Giver have planned for him before he ventured into the Unknown once again?

At that moment, a group of children charged down the hill toward him. "Ordinary! Ordinary!" they shouted excitedly. "Everyone is looking for you! You must come to the center of town! Hurry!"

"Why?" asked Ordinary. "What's going on?"

But the children just laughed, pulling him along behind them. Just before they reached the town square, IdeaMan, an Anybody who worked with Ordinary, approached them.

"Come quickly!' said IdeaMan, with a sly grin on his face. "I don't think you'll believe your eyes!"

There were so many people gathered in one spot that Ordinary could not make out what was happening. Then suddenly his father and mother stood before him, tired and dusty from their long but successful journey from the Land of Familiar. Ordinary threw his arms around Mom as Dad embraced them both.

For a long moment, tears of joy said it all. Then Dad stood back and said, "My son, you look. . . I don't know, the same, and yet you look completely different!"

"Yes, but you look so thin, my boy," Mom said. "Don't they feed you in this place?"

Ordinary laughed as he released his mother. "Of course, Mom!" Just then he became aware of someone standing behind Mom. She looked familiar, but he couldn't quite place her.

"You remember Little Molly, don't you?" asked Mom as she gently pushed this lovely creature toward her son. "She drafts Dreams and has come along to help people see their Big Dream through her pictures."

Just then, Ordinary recalled the Dream Giver's words, *One more thing is needed, and then you can go.* His heart began to beat faster as he wondered, *Could this be the "one thing"?*

∽

Many months passed as Little Molly worked together with Ordinary and his parents in the City of Anybodies. Ordinary had almost forgotten his impatience to move on. He couldn't believe the difference Little Molly's Dream Drawings made in the lives of those who had lost hope of ever pursuing their Big Dream. Watching her work inspired him. And he was amazed by her discernment as she placed her drawings in the hands of would-be dreamers at just the right moment.

"You two are made for each other!" joked IdeaMan. "She barely speaks a word, and you can't stop talking."

It was obvious to Ordinary that Mom favored Little Molly, but he couldn't make out what Dad thought of this new relationship. One day he summoned up the courage to ask him.

"I think you and Little Molly are right for each other, Ordinary," answered Dad. "But it's not what I think that's most important, is it?"

"You mean it's my own choice?"

"Is it? Your choice, I mean?"

Dad said nothing further. That night, when Ordinary thought back to his father's words, he was struck by this thought: He had been so excited over Little Molly that he had never asked the Dream Giver what He wanted! He walked through the city and once again stepped outside the walls. The landscape, stretching out before him, was breathtaking in the moonlight. He felt ashamed. How could he have neglected to seek the Dream Giver about his feelings for Little Molly?

Suddenly, Ordinary became aware of the Dream Giver's presence.

She is my Dream for you, spoke the Dream Giver softly, *and you are my Dream for her. You will share the rest of your Dream Journey together. It will be more difficult than you think, but I will be with you. It will also be more wonderful than you can imagine.*

∾

Not long after that, Ordinary and Little Molly were married, much to the delight of everyone in the City of Anybodies. After the celebration feast, Ordinary walked with his bride outside the city walls to gaze into the star-filled sky. Little Molly took something from her pocket and handed it to Ordinary. It was one of her Dream Drawings.

"The day you asked me to marry you," she said, "I drew this picture."

Ordinary looked at the picture and saw Little Molly at her drawing board. Behind her stood Ordinary, his hand on her shoulder, looking far into distant lands.

"I wish the picture showed what you were drawing," he said.

"No, I definitely felt that it wasn't for us to know. We'll have to discover it one step at a time. The Dream Giver has promised to be with us, and He will be faithful to show us the way."

Ordinary smiled at his new wife, who was the "one more thing" he definitely needed in his life. "It seems to me," he whispered, "that you should no longer be called Little Molly."

She laughed. "Just call me Wonder Molly, because you are often going to wonder what's going on in my mind. And I have a new name for you, too."

"Really? What's wrong with Ordinary?"

"Nothing." She smiled up at him. "But to me, you'll always be Extraordinary!"

The Dream Giver was right, thought Ordinary. *This is more wonderful than I imagined.*

CHAPTER TWO

COMFORT ZONE

As the months passed, Ordinary agreed that Wonder Molly was just the right name for his wife. She was truly a wonder as she managed their household and always knew precisely what he needed. She worked alongside him, and her gentle and quiet spirit always created a loving and peaceful atmosphere in their home. To tell the truth, Ordinary felt so content that he no longer awaited a sign from the Dream Giver to show them a new direction. Ordinary began to wonder whether they should not simply stay in the City of Anybodies.

Upon returning home one day, Ordinary was startled to find one of Wonder Molly's drawings on the table. It was a picture of them, knapsacks over their shoulders and on their way somewhere. Behind them stood the gateway to the City of Anybodies. In the gateway stood Mom weeping, with Dad waving.

"What sort of drawing is this?" asked Ordinary in an irritated tone, as Wonder Molly came in the door.

"I think it's time."

"Time for what?" His voice grew louder. "To leave Mom and Dad again? And all my work here? We have just settled down and you want us to go who knows where!"

Wonder Molly walked to the table and spread her hands protectively over her drawing.

Ordinary grew more furious. "For the first time in years I have a little peace and rest. I thought you were happy, but now I realize you feel nothing for me!"

He could see that his words hurt her deeply, but something within drove him to speak even more harshly. At last, she turned around and rushed out of the room. He heard the bedroom door slam and the key turn in the lock.

Ordinary went to stand in front of the locked door and shouted, "I thought you were not the sort of woman who would dictate what I should do!"

To his surprise, she opened the door.

"I never thought I would say this," she said softly, "but you're talking today just like my father." The door closed, this time in his face.

Ordinary was in shock. He, just like Difficult Dad? He stomped out of the house and headed straight to his parents' home.

After he had poured out the details of his story, Mom said, "Don't worry, dear. Mom will make it right for you.

To think she says you're like that scoundrel of a Difficult Dad! I'll tell her a thing or two, you can be sure of that."

"You'll do nothing of the sort!" said Dad. "This is not your problem, and they'll find their own solution."

"But—"

"No buts! Have you forgotten the commitment we made years ago? When our child marries, we must remember to let him go so that he can stand on his own feet. If we continue to sort out his problems, how do you think he'll learn to work things out?

"And you, my young man," he said, turning to Ordinary, "what do you mean by running to us like a toddler? Go home to your wife!"

Meandering down the dusty road, Ordinary felt as if his world had come to an end. Why did Wonder Molly want to complicate their lives? And how could Dad chase him out of the house as if it were his fault? But deep within his heart, another voice spoke. *How could you have talked to her that way? And how could you have continued when you saw how hurt she was?*

Suddenly a soft light encircled him. He realized that the Dream Giver was very close to him. His heart sank to his shoes. What would he say to the Dream Giver, now that his marriage was in such turmoil?

However, he didn't need to say anything. The next instant, he was overwhelmed by a Great Love that poured into him.

Go back and love Wonder Molly as I love you.

"But I—"

I said it would be harder than you thought, and more wonderful. Trust Me and go back!

◈

Wonder Molly, sitting at the table, looked up as he came in, but said nothing.

"I'm...I'm sorry," Ordinary said. "I behaved badly and..."

Wonder Molly set down her drawing and stood up. "I don't understand why you were so upset. I thought you would be encouraged by the sketch. I believe it's the sign you've been seeking."

"It's just that I feel so...comfortable here."

"Perhaps it's time to leave our Comfort Zone and venture out to live our next Big Dream," Wonder Molly said.

Ordinary was tempted to become angry again, but then he realized what she said was true.

"And it's not just about the drawing," Wonder Molly went on. "It seems to me that you are also in a Comfort Zone in our relationship. I try to talk to you but you only hear half of what I say. And the one time I attempt to tell you what I believe, you become angry. You won't allow me to come close to you...and after what happened today, I feel as though I can't even be honest with you."

Ordinary thought his heart would break. He heard again the voice in his heart. *Go back and love Wonder Molly as I love you.*

"I'm sorry," he said, genuinely this time, and walked toward his wife. He saw the tears in her eyes and held out his arms to her. "Will you forgive me?"

Ordinary saw her nod as she flung her arms around him. Then he heard the voice again, clear and precise, *It is time.*

CHAPTER THREE

BORDERLAND

The following day, Ordinary invited his father and mother to come for dinner. He also invited IdeaMan so he would be there for the great announcement.

"Wonder Molly and I have come to realize that the Dream Giver wants us to go toward another Big Dream."

"Another dream?" IdeaMan asked. "But what of our food project? These Never-Ending Gardens are feeding thousands of Anybodies and—"

"I've just arrived here!" Mom exclaimed. "I can't go following after you again!"

Dad just laughed and said, "Dear me, woman, what are you talking about? I didn't hear Ordinary inviting us along!"

"How will the two of you survive so far away from us?" Mom asked.

"After yesterday, I wonder how they would have survived so close to us," said Dad, attempting to lighten the conversation.

"I can't believe how selfish you are," IdeaMan said. "You just want to go off on adventures, but you forget your work is here."

Back and forth they argued and sought to convince Ordinary and Wonder Molly that what they wanted to do was a complete mistake.

At long last, Wonder Molly broke in. "I think my husband has done an excellent job at answering your questions and concerns. I trust him completely and will follow him wherever he chooses to go."

Ordinary felt his buttons pop at his wife's confidence in him.

"We've talked enough for now," Wonder Molly continued. "We believe we must go, and that's that."

Mom sniffled. "Well, you can see who's boss in this house."

"Ordinary, you can't plan your future on a woman's paltry drawings!" IdeaMan said.

"My wife is the number one person in my life," Ordinary said. "If we don't take this journey together, it will be the biggest mistake we make. But in any case, we're not going because I want to or because she wants to. We're going because the Dream Giver will have it so."

"Then that settles it," replied Dad. "It's your life and your marriage, so we have no other choice than to support you in it."

Mom was silent. IdeaMan looked as though he wanted to speak but refrained.

A short time later, everyone said their good-byes and left Ordinary and Wonder Molly alone.

"Wow," Ordinary sighed in relief.

"You can say that again," Wonder Molly said.

❧

When they left the City of Anybodies a few days later, Mom stood weeping while Dad waved.

"One thing I know after these last few days," Wonder Molly said. "I really am more important to you than your parents or your friends."

Ordinary smiled. "And the truth is, our marriage is *our* marriage. It's good we're taking this journey on our own."

"I can hardly wait to get started," Wonder Molly said. "It feels as though nothing can go wrong for us, ever again."

CHAPTER FOUR

WASTELAND

everal weeks into their journey, Ordinary and
Wonder Molly found themselves taking paths that led
nowhere. Time after time they had to backtrack and start
over in a different direction. Their energy and patience
were wearing thin.

One night, as they lay in each other's arms, looking at
the stars, Wonder Molly whispered, "I hadn't anticipated
the journey's being so hard. It feels as though nothing we
do goes right and we're wasting our time day after day."

They slept fitfully that night. The next morning when
they awoke, the sun was already above the horizon.

"Please get my hairbrush for me," Wonder Molly

teased. "Otherwise I'll look like the wild woman of Borneo all day."

Ordinary got up but couldn't see their things. Strange footprints were evident where their knapsacks had been placed the night before.

"Our things have been stolen!" he yelled.

"Wha...what?" she said, sitting straight up and fully awake.

"The bags have been stolen from right here, where you left them lying."

"Where *I* left them lying?" she said. "You were the last person to get something out, remember?"

For several minutes they threw angry accusations back and forth until...

"Wait, let's not fight," Ordinary said. "We must follow the thief."

"But he could be dangerous," Wonder Molly protested.

Ordinary had already chosen his course, and she had no option but to follow. She grabbed up their sleeping bags and set off after him. *If I don't look after our belongings,* she thought, *we'll have nothing.*

For an hour or so, Wonder Molly tried hard to follow Ordinary, but he was running too fast. Finally she sat down, exhausted, under a weird, knotted tree. She looked around and didn't like what she saw. Then suddenly, a long dark shadow fell over her.

"I lost the trail," said Ordinary, who had doubled back and now stood behind her. "It's hopeless."

"What are we going to do? Everything was in our bags! We have nothing. No food, no money..." Then, looking around, Wonder Molly added, "And I don't like this place!"

Ordinary looked at their surroundings more carefully and then at the tree she sat under. It was a struggling tree.

They were in WasteLand!

That entire day they plodded through a dry desert section of WasteLand. Ordinary found a small amount of water, somewhat bitter, and a piece of fruit, somewhat sour.

Wonder Molly was quiet. Ordinary tried to cheer her up with one of his childhood stories, but she did not respond. He became irritated at her silence. He remembered what IdeaMan said, "She barely speaks a word and you can't stop talking." Up until then, her silence had been one of her finer qualities. Now he couldn't tolerate it. Was she blaming him because they were lost? He didn't know what she was thinking. "You're often going to wonder what goes on in my mind," she had once joked with him.

That night they went to sleep tired and hungry, with the sour taste of WasteLand's meager fruit in their mouths. When they awoke the following morning, the desert wind was blowing sand everywhere.

"I can't stand it anymore!" cried Wonder Molly. "Everything's gone—my drawings, my hairbrush, everything! Now this miserable sandstorm. And I just want. . . to brush my hair!"

She dissolved into tears, and Ordinary sat with his arms around her and remained silent.

Much later, they stood up and continued to walk along in silence. The wind became so strong that they could barely see. Suddenly Wonder Molly tripped and fell forward. Ordinary grabbed her just in time. As he steadied her, they both looked down wide-eyed at what was on the ground.

There lay a young boy. His eyes were closed and he was barely breathing. Ordinary could only imagine how long he had been wandering aimlessly through this strange WasteLand. Ordinary's last ounce of courage left him. The boy would not be able to take a single step, yet they couldn't leave him here. Ordinary would have to carry him, though it would make their journey that much harder.

To his amazement, Wonder Molly immediately knelt down by the boy, her tears and complaints forgotten. "Come," she said, "we must carry him. If you could just carry him awhile, I will try to gather some fruit. And when you're tired, I'll take him."

All that day they struggled with the boy, until both felt they could go no farther. They struggled to carry him, they struggled with their fatigue, and they struggled with their fears. Suppose the boy died, here in WasteLand. What would they do then?

Exhausted, they finally found shelter in an old abandoned mine and fell into a deep sleep.

∾

The next morning they both awoke, anxious to see if the boy had made it through the night. To their surprise, he was awake and sitting at the entrance to the mine.

"My name is DreamGuide," he said with an embarrassed smile. "I had a Dream in which I helped people through WasteLand, and then I became lost myself. I realize now that it was a silly Dream. I am far too young and WasteLand is far too big. Besides—"

"Wait!" Wonder Molly exclaimed. "I want to make a drawing for you."

Ordinary looked at her in amazement. What could she use to draw? But, bending down, she drew with her finger on the smooth sand floor. DreamGuide looked over her shoulder, spellbound.

"Can that be?" he asked.

"Yes," Wonder Molly answered. "You were sent to lead us to Sanctuary, but you had to cross our path in the way you did so that we would carry you. With you as our DreamGuide through WasteLand, we had to learn to share our burden."

DreamGuide looked up in wonderment. "I can't believe it. I had no idea where we were, but now I do! Sanctuary is scarcely half a day's walk from here."

Later that day, worn out and limping along, Ordinary and Wonder Molly entered the lush green forest leading to Sanctuary. They turned to wave good-bye to DreamGuide, but he was already well on his way back to WasteLand to help other Dreamers.

CHAPTER FIVE

SANCTUARY

*W*hat an amazing encounter they had in Sanctuary. It didn't take long for their weariness from WasteLand to disappear in the presence of the Dream Giver. Every day Ordinary and Wonder Molly strolled hand in hand along the flowing streams and climbed the magnificent mountain peaks.

One evening they sat beside the still water of a crystal clear pool, taking in the beauty all around them. They both were thinking about how bad they looked and felt when they first arrived at Sanctuary.

"It seems to me," Wonder Molly said, breaking the silence, "that one must first experience real dirt and tiredness to understand how great it feels to plunge into the Dream Giver's refreshing waters."

Ordinary nodded. "I never knew that spending time together in the Dream Giver's presence would do such wonders for our relationship. And my time alone with Him really restores my soul." He turned to Wonder Molly and knew that she, too, had been to the Light.

"The Dream Giver's Light is so penetrating," she said. "I understood for the first time how difficult my silence was for you. I thought remaining quiet would make it easier for you in WasteLand. But in the Light, I realized that silence can be selfish and harmful to our Dream."

"It wasn't easy to see into my own heart either," Ordinary said, "but the Dream Giver's Light brings freedom from all kinds of darkness. It also helped me say 'I'm sorry' to you for all the times I've blown it."

Smiling, he took Wonder Molly's hand in his as she laid her head on his shoulder. For the next few moments they enjoyed the renewal they both were experiencing.

Then Wonder Molly said quietly, "I made an interesting discovery while here in Sanctuary."

"I think I know what it is. We've both come to realize that the Dream Giver must come first in our lives...even before each other. Am I right?"

"Yes," she answered. "He gently asked me to give you back to Him last night, and I have a feeling He asked the same of you."

The more they talked about their Compassionate Friend, the more they sensed He was waiting for them at the Summit. As Ordinary and Wonder Molly helped each other scale the steep rock face of the mountain, it became obvious that they were touching holy ground.

They reached the very top of the Summit just as a dark cloud covered the face of the sun. All they could see was a massive altar with something brightly burning on it. As they approached the flames, it became obvious what was being sacrificed.

"No!" Wonder Molly screamed as she ran toward the fire. Ordinary had to restrain her from reaching into the flames. They clung to one another, tears streaming down their faces, as they watched in disbelief.

"How could Dream Giver do such a thing?" questioned Ordinary.

Every hope, plan, and dream they had together was turning to ashes right before their eyes. Then came that gentle voice:

Will you give it all to Me? the Dream Giver asked.

Wonder Molly sobbed. "I can't live without Ordinary, and I don't want to sacrifice our marriage and everything we have together."

As she wept, Ordinary's eyes rested on one of the stones in the middle of the altar. Bending down, he saw the inscribed words and slowly read out loud:

"Most assuredly, I say to you, unless a grain of wheat falls into the ground and dies, it remains alone; but if it dies, it produces much grain."

Wonder Molly slowly knelt beside her husband and read the words over and over. "Now I remember," she said, wiping the tears from her cheeks.

Ordinary's puzzled expression encouraged her to go on.

"Last night, when He asked us to release each other into His hands, I sensed there was more He wanted us to know."

"It's not just about giving up each other, is it?" Ordinary said.

"No, He wants us to love Him more than we love each other or our Dream marriage. . .even our very lives!"

Once again the question came: *Will you give it all to Me?*

Kneeling before the burning altar, Ordinary and Wonder Molly pledged their love and loyalty to the Dream Giver alone. He was worthy, and when they finished. . .everything was His.

They looked up and noticed the flames were no longer burning. There on the altar lay the most beautiful sight—the marriage of their Dreams. The fire had not consumed it, only refined it.

Suddenly, Ordinary and Wonder Molly felt surrounded by Greatness. The Dream Giver had taken their Dream only to give it back to them again. As they descended the mountain, their Dream tucked securely in their hearts, the Dream Giver spoke one last time:

Live the marriage of your Dreams. . .the harvest is yet to come.

◦∾◦

The following morning, both Ordinary and Wonder Molly knew they were ready to continue their journey. They were different people as a result of their time spent in Sanctuary. They felt refreshed, rejuvenated, and ready for the rest of their journey to the Land of Promise.

VALLEY OF GIANTS

*L*ater that day, Ordinary and Wonder Molly made their way along a steep and rugged road that descended into the Valley of Giants. They rounded a bend, and stopped dead in their tracks.

"Oh, no. Not him!" Ordinary's voice trembled when he saw a massive Giant lying in their path.

"Do you recognize him?" asked Wonder Molly.

"Yes. His name is Moneyless. He's one of the largest and most dangerous Giants in the valley."

"I've heard about him, but he doesn't look all that scary. Besides, we're a team and we can take him!" Then to Ordinary's utter shock, Wonder Molly let out a war cry and ran at the Giant ready to fight.

"Wait, wait!" cried Ordinary, running after her. "You can't fight the Giant by yourself!"

Wonder Molly spun around and Ordinary ran into her, knocking them both to the ground.

"Well, then," she said in a frustrated tone, "come help me!"

"You don't understand. It's good to have the courage to fight, but Giants are so large that, alone, we are powerless against them. Don't you remember what we learned in Sanctuary?"

Sitting by the side of the road, Ordinary reminded Wonder Molly that the Dream Giver promised to be with them throughout their journey. "But He also said, 'Call to Me, and I will answer you, and show you great and mighty things.'"

"Well, that looks like a 'great and mighty thing' to me," she said, pointing to the Giant, who was now heading their way.

"Then we better start calling!" Ordinary shouted over the roar of the beast coming fast toward them.

Together they cried out to the Dream Giver as Ordinary braced himself to protect Wonder Molly.

Then the most amazing thing happened. Just as the Giant was about to grab Ordinary and Wonder Molly up in his hands, his eyes caught sight of Something behind them and he stood motionless. He gave them one frightened look and then charged away with huge strides out of the valley.

"I have never felt so frightened in my life," Wonder Molly said, "nor so protected!"

Without a word between them, they dropped to their knees, thanking the Dream Giver for answering their call. The victory over the Giant was His and His alone.

By the time their journey through the Valley of Giants was over, they had witnessed the miraculous. Every encounter with their Giants had been won, not by their power or strength, but by their faith in the Dream Giver.

CHAPTER SEVEN

THE LAND OF PROMISE

"We're almost there!" Ordinary exclaimed as they crested the hill and stood overlooking the Land of Promise. Before them lay their City of Dreams with its white marble walls and golden domes glistening in the sun.

Wonder Molly stood next to Ordinary and said, "How beautiful!"

"It looks so...perfect," Ordinary said. "But what sort of needs would anyone have living in such a lovely place? Is this the way you pictured it?"

"No," Wonder Molly said. "But knowing the Dream Giver as we do, He'll reveal His plan for us only one step at a time."

It wasn't long before they reached the city gates. The moment they stepped inside, everything looked different. The walls inside the city were cracked and didn't look anything like marble. The domes no longer glistened, but looked discolored and in need of repair.

The streets were littered with trash. Everywhere they looked, they saw evidence that no one cared. Everything had been neglected, and although there were lots of stores and houses, no one was in sight. There were no sounds of children anywhere.

"The whole place looks abandoned," Wonder Molly said. "Are you sure this is where the Dream Giver wanted us to come?"

"Quite sure," Ordinary replied.

As the day wore on, Ordinary discovered a boardinghouse where they could stay for the night. The plush, comfortable bed was a nice change from sleeping on the ground in the valley.

"It's strange," Wonder Molly whispered in the darkness. "I feel so at home in our new surroundings."

And without another word, they both fell asleep.

◈

Sometime in the middle of the night, Wonder Molly awoke to the sound of a faint cry. She quietly slipped out of bed and into the next room. Looking around, she found some paper and pencils. It had been a long time since she had drawn a picture, and she sat down and began to draw.

There it was again. . .the sound of someone crying.

She went to the window, but all was quiet, so she went back to her drawing. She finished her work and then made herself comfortable on the sofa. The next thing she knew, Ordinary was smiling down at her with the drawing in his hand.

"This is magnificent!" he told her excitedly. "And it matches perfectly with the dream I had last night."

For hours they talked and planned how they could best meet the Great Need they had discovered.

That afternoon they knocked on door after door. Every home they entered looked exactly like Wonder Molly's drawing—a husband and wife sitting on opposite sides of a lovely upholstered bench, looking away from each other.

"There are many couples in this needy city who have given up on each other," Ordinary said to Wonder Molly.

"Can't you just imagine the difference it will make," Wonder Molly said, "when they learn what the Dream Giver has taught us! If we can learn to live the marriage of our dreams, so can they."

And with that, they continued on with their Big Plans to meet the Great Need in their Land of Promise. Little did they know, the Harvest was yet to come!

PART II

THE JOURNEY TO THE MARRIAGE OF YOUR DREAMS

CHAPTER EIGHT

THE DREAM

*Avoid the Cinderella syndrome and
accept God's perspective on marriage.*

And they lived happily ever after.

After what? What did Cinderella and her Prince Charming have to go through before they could live happily? That part of the story has never been told.

Picture the final scene. An exceptional-looking bride and her groom wrap their arms around each other, jump into a waiting carriage, and ride off into Fantasyland as the words *The End* come up on the screen. Every little girl sits there with a smile on her face and the hope in her heart that someday *her* Prince Charming will come and take her off to live happily ever after, too. Every little boy (eventually) longs for the day when he will discover the girl of his dreams. The problem is, no one has told them that "the end" of the story is just the *beginning*.

When Prince Charming and Cinderella awaken the following morning, they embark on a journey together that would be a sequel *really* worth watching.

Can't you just picture Cinderella, without any makeup, complaining that Prince Charming has left the toilet seat up again? How would you like to have a king and queen for in-laws, trying to live up to their expectations? And how do you ever get time alone when everyone—including the press—is watching you? How sensitive was the prince to his young bride, and did Cinderella ever get jealous when another princess looked at her attractive husband?

Think about your own wedding day. How convinced were you that this person you were marrying was going to be the answer to all your dreams? How high were your expectations that nothing and no one would ever be able to hinder the love you both felt at that moment? How long did the "honeymoon" last? Months? Weeks? Days?

AFTER THE HONEYMOON

I will never forget the day Bruce said something I didn't expect to hear in a million years. We had been married only a few months when I started to get really annoyed that my new Prince Charming was less attentive than I thought he should be. Part of the problem with the Cinderella syndrome is that you believe the person you marry will be the source of your every fulfillment and joy.

The tension between us became so great that, finally,

my frustrated new husband blurted out, "I don't *want* to be responsible for *your* happiness."

You could have knocked me over with my glass slipper! I was shocked, hurt, and outraged. *Well, thank you very much. Why didn't you tell me that* before *I married you?*

I didn't realize it at the time, but Bruce was expressing to me that the burden I had placed on him was too heavy. He entered into this arrangement expecting to take on the role of my husband, not my God. You see, I thought Bruce had been created for the sole purpose of meeting my every need. Poor guy!

And because Bruce was unable to live up to my picture of the perfect spouse, I was unhappy.

We can laugh about it today, but at the time it wasn't funny at all.

Marriage is meant to be the most wonderful, satisfying, and fulfilling of all human relationships this side of heaven. The good news is, since it is meant to be the marriage of your dreams, there must be a way to get there.

THE HEAVENLY UNION

The Bible tells us after life on earth is over and God's people have joined Him for eternity, "they neither marry nor are given in marriage, but are like angels of God in heaven" (Matthew 22:30). You see, God's idea for marriage is a man and woman coming together to accomplish something wonderful while they are here on planet earth. The problem begins when we try to fill in the blanks on our own.

If someone had asked you on your wedding day, "Why are you getting married?" what would you have said?

"We're in love."

"We want to have sex."

"We plan to have a family."

"We're made for each other."

"We believe we'll do better together than we will apart."

All good reasons to tie the knot, but are they what God had in mind when He first presented Adam with the one and only woman in his life? Let's consider the original story.

The invention of marriage took place in the Garden of Eden. According to the account in Genesis 2, God placed the man Adam, whom He had created, into a garden and gave him certain instructions. One of Adam's first responsibilities was to give a name to every living creature. What a job that must have been! Can't you just hear Adam laughing when he encountered some of God's more creative creatures? How many months do you suppose it would take to examine and name every living thing God made?

In the midst of Adam's work, God made a very interesting observation: "For Adam there was not found a helper comparable to him" (Genesis 2:20). God decided, "It is not good that man should be alone; I will make him a helper comparable to him" (v. 18). Someone to help complete the job.

What an awesome God! Here was His perfect human being doing exactly what God had asked him to do. Creator and His creation were in complete harmony.

Adam's fellowship with God must have been beyond our comprehension as they conversed and delighted in one another. Adam was never completely "alone," and yet something "not good" tugs at the heart of God. He observes that Adam has no one to work alongside and experience this new life together. He needs someone to identify with on a human level. Someone must be created for Adam, not only to assist him in accomplishing the many things God wants done, but to be a delightful reminder of God's unselfish desire to see Adam fulfilled in a special relationship with someone else.

For years I have been fascinated by the way God went about creating this first woman, Eve. He could have done it exactly the way He made Adam, but He didn't. Perhaps He wanted the man and the woman to forever remember the great care He took in fashioning this special woman for the unique purpose of coming alongside this man for the rest of their lives.

Fortunately, Adam didn't miss the significance of this woman, who, I am sure, looked far superior to the animals he had been naming all day. Listen to his excited response to her:

> "This is now bone of my bones
> And flesh of my flesh;
> She shall be called Woman,
> Because she was taken out of Man."
>
> GENESIS 2:23

Adam must have been overwhelmed at the sight of Eve. When was the last time you said, "Wow, look what

I've been given!"? (I'm talking about your spouse, not a piece of dessert.) Do you feel like a special person to your husband? Do you see your wife as a special person from God? That kind of response comes as a result of choices you make. But we'll talk about that later.

LEAVE TO CLEAVE

The Bible goes on to say, "Therefore a man shall leave his father and mother and be joined to his wife, and they shall become one flesh" (Genesis 2:24). Imagine a bewildered Eve wondering, "What's a. . .*mother?*"

"I don't know," Adam replies. "What's a *father?*"

Of course, they had neither mother nor father, so God's inspired Word includes this verse for all time for married couples to understand something significant: *The marriage relationship is meant to be worth leaving home for.*

Marriage is to take priority over even the strongest blood relationship. Husband and wife are joined together, united, connected as "one flesh." Sounds as if God really wants you as a couple to stick together in a most intimate way. And it requires you to cut the apron strings in order to accomplish it.

Several years ago, Bruce and I taught a seminar on marriage. We shared the importance of a couple's choosing to leave in order to cleave to each other in marriage. During a break, a young woman approached us in tears and said, "My husband and I have been married for five years. Last year he received a job offer in another state, but I refused to move and leave my parents. Now I understand why our marriage has suffered. I apologized to my husband for clinging to my family instead of to him."

Just then, her husband came up and embraced her and thanked us for enabling them to be rejoined in their relationship. Their decision to leave their hometown would be difficult, but they were focused on reconnecting as man and wife.

If this young wife had not made the decision to leave, what might their relationship have become over the years? Not this, I hope:

> One afternoon, an elderly couple was invited to their neighbors' for tea. The hostess asked the husband if he took sugar in his tea. He replied no at the exact time his wife, in an attempt to answer for him, said, "Yes!" Looking indignantly at him, the wife chided, "I always put sugar in your tea." The old gentlemen sighed. "I know. I used to tell you not to, but now I just don't stir."

All of us have been around a couple who seem to be as sensitive to each other as a mother ostrich who hides her precious egg and then, moments later, steps on it. Marriage is too precious and life's too short not to do whatever's necessary to be a loving, caring couple that everyone wants to be like.

But you don't wake up after fifty years of marriage loving each other when you haven't been willing over the years to take the journey to make it the marriage of your dreams. What exactly can you do today, tomorrow, and in the days ahead to start down the yellow brick road with the rainbow at the other end? Wouldn't it be wonderful to someday hear your spouse say, "Of all the people in the entire world, I am so glad I married you!" (and really mean it)? We suggest three things that we hope will give you a jump start to having that dream come true.

THREE STEPS TO BEGIN YOUR JOURNEY

1. Discover the secrets of a marriage created in heaven.

We're all familiar with the expression "made for each other" and have no trouble believing it on our wedding day. But it doesn't take long after the honeymoon to discover that this marriage made in heaven must be worked out here on earth. Bruce and I never liked the idea that we had to work at our marriage. However, "working on the marriage of your dreams" has a much nicer sound. So let's take that approach.

Developing the marriage of your dreams is a lifelong process that takes time and commitment. Regardless of how much you love your spouse, you still come into marriage with different backgrounds, different parents, different experiences, and different ways of looking at things. So why are we so shocked to find that in order to live the marriage of our dreams, we must seek and make choices that will enable us to reach our goal?

Where did your concept of a marriage made in heaven come from? A television sitcom, your parents or grandparents, your newly married friends? When Bruce and I said, "I do," we had never taken a course on how to be happily married. Here we faced a lifelong relationship, and the only preparation we had was what we came up with in our imaginations. Have you ever tried to live up to someone's expectations?

For instance, some spouses grow up in a family where the mother wears the pants. I remember the night Bruce and I discovered from the Bible that the husband is the head of the wife as Christ is the head of the church. We began to look into this teaching and uncovered some life-changing truths:

1. God designated the husband, not the wife, as the head.
2. This choice was not based on who was more intelligent or gifted.
3. The man must fulfill the role as head in order for the marriage to work.
4. The wife is to be subject to her husband as the church is to Christ.

Over the months that followed we discovered that as we brought our marriage in line with God's perfect plan, we saw amazing results. A husband looks to his wife to talk through difficult issues, to encourage him when he is down, to listen to his ideas and plans, to meet his sexual needs, to assist him and work alongside him in accomplishing God's purposes. However, when a man's position as head is constantly challenged or usurped by his wife, he will not be inclined or motivated to fulfill his role as husband.

The same is true for the wife. Her role is not to be her husband's servant or maid, but his life partner. She is to assist him to accomplish things he could not accomplish alone. Sometimes that means giving him good advice or sharing the truth with him in a particular situation. Sometimes a wife understands that she and her husband need to have a quiet meal together without the children around or to spend a morning alone after a hard week's work. God made a woman especially sensitive and nurturing because she is needed to be the support system to the most important man in her life.

Some couples believe the lie that fulfillment comes from living a life that's independent and separate from each other. The exact opposite is true. When you actively seek to fulfill the role God has given you as a husband or wife, you will be in for some surprising adventures.

During the early years of our marriage, Bruce wanted to become a better teacher. I would go along with him whenever he was invited to speak, and he was always so well received. After he spoke, the people would swarm around him, eager to express their appreciation. On one occasion, as I stood there hearing all these wonderful compliments, I decided it was my job as a good wife to keep him humble. So on the way home, I read him my list of criticisms. I could tell that he seemed to be discouraged about the job he had done.

Imagine my surprise when I opened my Amplified Bible the following morning to Ephesians 5:33 and read God's expectation for a wife:

Let the wife see that she respects and reverences her husband—that she notices him, regards him, honors him, prefers him, venerates, and esteems him; and that she defers to him, praises him, and loves and admires him exceedingly.

AMP

I was shocked! Rather than shooting him down, my job was to build him up. There's a time and place to give my honest evaluation, but not when he's most vulnerable. Right after he speaks is the time to share what he did well.

Bruce's expectations of being a good husband had to change also. He read and meditated on "husbands, love your wives, just as Christ also loved the church and gave Himself for her" (Ephesians 5:25). Like many husbands, he thought he was to love me only if he felt it or if I deserved it. His actions and responses began to change as he realized that loving was a choice he could make regardless of my response.

Over the years, we have discovered God's marriage manual, the Bible, constantly puts our relationship back on track. It's the compass that keeps us going in the right direction toward the marriage of our dreams.

Here's an interesting exercise for you to do together:

A. Look in your Bible's concordance and write down all the passages on wives, husbands, and marriage.
B. Read and discuss these verses together, asking God to reveal where you are in tune or out of tune with His instructions.
C. Choose one area you can improve in and commit to help each other.

2. *Seek to fulfill each other's dreams in your marriage.*

Everyone has a dream in their heart, and chances are pretty good that the two of you have similar dreams for your relationship, your family, and your life. Talk about these dreams together and how you want to pursue them. Whatever you do, don't let only one of you have all the dreams. If your spouse doesn't know of a dream he wants to pursue, take the initiative to help him come up with one. Even a small dream is worth planning for and celebrating. Perhaps one of your dreams as a couple is to take an overseas missions trip. Planning how to raise the funds, praying, and preparing for the trip together can be an unforgettable memory.

There are also dreams that are unique to you as an individual. It is so important that you allow your spouse to have a dream that may not be a shared dream. A friend of mine began her own candy store, which was a childhood dream. Her husband encouraged her and gave her good advice about legal matters. However, he celebrated her success and did not insist that he manage the business. Your husband may have a dream to climb the tallest mountain in your area. You, on the other hand, get a nosebleed climbing the stairs. It's fine for you to encourage him to fulfill his dream without having to purchase hiking boots and accompany him.

What an adventure you will have as a married couple as you help one another discover some dreams and then look for ways to help those dreams come true. Imagine what great times of reminiscing you will have about all the ways you assisted one another to have a more exciting and enjoyable life. Don't forget to develop a good sense of humor as you seek to see a dream become a reality. Never laugh at your spouse's dream even if you think it's a silly idea. Remember this good instruction: "Be kindly affectionate to one another with brotherly love, in honor giving preference to one another" (Romans 12:10).

∽

Her husband was a musician who traveled from town to town playing the violin to make a living. He had not been doing well. Times were hard, and there was little money for common folk to come to hear the musician, even though he was a brilliant player and his fee was small. At last he had to let his accompanist go. His wife, who could play the piano fairly well, started to practice diligently so that she could accompany him. She knew that performing music was a necessity of life to him. His dream was to play before kings, and she wanted to do all she could to support his dream.

One evening, shortly before his performance in the city hall of a small town, he said dejectedly that he saw no reason for opening that night. A storm was raging outside. "Who will venture out on a night like this?" he asked. "Last night we performed for just a handful. Even fewer will come tonight. Why not give back the meager fees of those who bought those few tickets and cancel the concert? No one can expect us to go on when just a few are in the audience."

In her dismay his wife did not know what to answer.

"How can anyone do his best for so few?" he went on. Finally, she looked straight at him. "I know you're discouraged, but you're an artist and you can bring joy to those few who come to listen to you. We will go on. And we will do the best job we're capable of. It's not the fault of those who come that others do not. They shouldn't be punished with less than the best we can give."

Heartened by her words, the violinist agreed to go ahead with their show. They had never performed better. When the show was over, the small audience gave a standing ovation and left. While the artist was gathering up his music, an older man, who looked vaguely familiar, gestured to the artist's wife to accompany him to the door. She returned beaming, with a note in her hand. She put her arm round her husband and said, "Listen to this, my love!" Slowly she read: "Thank you for a life-changing performance." It was signed very simply, "Your king."

She explained to her astounded husband that the royal listener was traveling incognito and happened to be staying in that town for the night. He loved the violin and attended the performance to pass the time.

By encouraging her husband not to give up his dream, the wife inadvertently helped him fulfill his dream of "playing before kings." Later, the king sponsored the talented young musician to get further training, and he become a renowned violinist.[1]

3. Reevaluate your Dream Marriage through the seasons of life.

The wonderful thing about dreams is that they surface throughout our entire lives. You start dreaming about things as a young couple, but those dreams will look entirely different from the ones you will pursue after you've been married thirty years. That's why it's so important that you grow in your understanding of each other's dreams and become more experienced dream makers as the years progress. One way to create the marriage of your dreams is to dream together.

After Bruce and I had been married over twenty years, we began talking about how quickly time seemed to pass. Then we thought about our parents, who had been married twice as long. All four of our parents were healthy and doing fine at that time, but we realized there would come a day when they wouldn't be as fit as they were at present. We began to dream and plan a couple of four-day trips that we could take separately with each couple. We knew the perfect place they would enjoy, so we made the arrangements and then the announcement.

They were delighted! The pictures we took and the memories we have of those two trips were well worth the time and money spent to see this dream become a reality.

One of the things we observed about our parents was the need to look forward to something as couples. Marriage can become stale and uninteresting in any season if you don't keep the dreams flowing. Attending an event you both enjoy, inviting people for dinner or games, scheduling a vacation with friends or family, doing ministry together, helping a widow in your neighborhood—these are examples of activities that you can look forward to together.

Take a moment and fast-forward yourself into the future. Picture you and your spouse five, ten, even twenty years from now. What will you want to be true about your relationship? What will be the characteristics of your dream marriage?

In order to make your dream come true, get ready to take a journey through the next stage that will enable you to unlock the door to living the marriage of your dreams.

---

1. Creative adaptation of a story, original author unknown.

CHAPTER NINE

COMFORT ZONES

PRINCIPLE #2
*Break through your Comfort Zone and
become transparent.*

Wonder Molly laid down her drawing and stood up. "I don't understand why you were so upset. I thought you would be encouraged by the sketch. I believe it's the sign you've been seeking."

"It's just that I feel so. . .comfortable here."

"Perhaps it's time to leave our Comfort Zone and venture out to live our next Big Dream," Wonder Molly said.

They looked absolutely miserable. In fact, everyone around the dinner table noticed that it almost seemed painful for them to be sitting next to each other. "What's wrong with Kim and Gregg?" whispered Lisa, Kim's younger sister. "I don't know," replied her husband, "but I sure hope it's not contagious." Kim and Gregg had been married almost ten years and Lisa had always admired their relationship. Their love and affection for each other was a constant example to Lisa and Brad, who had been married only a few months.

After the children were excused, Lisa and Kim found themselves alone in the kitchen putting away the leftovers.

"Can I ask you a question?" Lisa asked her sister.

"Sure," replied Kim, trying to avoid eye contact.

"Did you and Gregg have a fight or something?"

"I wish we had! How can you fight with someone who won't talk?"

Sound familiar? In case you think you and your spouse are the only couple who struggles with communication problems, let me tell you our story. During our first year of marriage, Darlene Marie and I were proud of the fact that we rarely had a disagreement. However, on a number of occasions, it became obvious to me that something was bothering her.

I came from a home where my dad and I would sit at the kitchen table for hours after everyone else had gone to bed and talk through all kinds of issues. Darlene Marie came from a family that easily conversed for hours over a game of cards or a puzzle, but rarely shared their deepest feelings. Therefore, our first conversations went something like this:

Husband: "Are you upset about something, sweetheart?"

Wife: "No."

Husband: "Are you sure?"

Wife: "Yeah." (Deep sigh.)

Husband: "Did I do something wrong?"

Wife: "Ummm. . .not really."

Husband: "Do you want to tell me about it?"

Wife: "I don't know."

This went on for a solid hour and then only sometimes would we finally uncover the reason for which we were not having a disagreement. Being married doesn't automatically make you an avid communicator. Wouldn't it be wonderful if, along with your marriage license, they also provided you and your spouse with a license to communicate! Then, regardless of your past, the moment you said "I do," you would be assured of never hearing your spouse say "I don't want to talk about it."

Unfortunately, many arrive at the threshold of the marriage of their dreams only to discover that they can't get past an invisible barrier. What is this invisible barrier, and why does it cause us to resemble a clam when it comes to sharing our true feelings?

FEELING COMFORTABLE?

Did your spouse ever say to you while you were dating, "I feel so comfortable with you"? Being a man, I know how that translates. It means just being in your presence is all I need. To a woman it means feeling safe and content. However, after the honeymoon, life must be lived in the real world. That requires you to sometimes leave this wonderful place called your comfort zone.

Let's face it. You love your comfort zone. It's where your slippers, your cozy recliner, and your cup of tea or coffee all reside. When you're in your comfort zone, all is right with your world. It is full of the routines that you are used to and it feels so good to remain in territory that you're familiar with and where you know it's safe. Since we all enjoy being comfortable, one of the last things you expect your marriage to do is make you uncomfortable.

At the very edge of your comfort zone is an invisible wall that every couple must face sooner or later. It's the wall of fear. It's always a fearful thing to go where you've never gone before. However, this wall must be scaled if you are to pursue the marriage of your dreams. What are some of these fears that a couple may encounter?

The fear of exposure. Even though you have a need to be loved and may believe that your spouse loves you, there is still the fear of being transparent. You think if you are totally honest about yourself, he or she may not love you. Therefore, it's safer to hide your true feelings and not risk the danger of being rejected.

The fear of the unknown. Everyone has experienced the stress of not wanting to confess a mistake because they weren't sure how their spouse would react. It's also unsettling to attempt something together you have never tried before. Not being sure of the outcome of a situation makes you want to curl up in your comfort zone rather than step into challenging areas.

The fear of intimacy. You want your relationship with your spouse to be fulfilling and intimate. Yet it is sometimes frightening to do and say things on a deeply personal level. It's one thing to share the same bed; it's quite another to share your hearts.

Every married couple will face the trauma of stepping

toward the edge of their comfort zone. Feelings of inadequacy and uncertainty can turn you back from exploring new territory. It's much easier to let your every conversation skim the surface than to take a chance on getting into deep waters where the real you resides. That's not to say that you can't enjoy many days of laughter and conversations that are purely fun. However, there must be moments when you take each other by the hand and choose to walk through your wall of fear.

In our opening story, Kim expressed her frustration with a problem many couples face. It may seem easy at first to share every experience with each other and to be able to talk about anything and everything. As time goes on, you can become so familiar with each other that you just assume your spouse knows how you feel and what you're thinking.

The comfort zone seems to caution you, "If it isn't broken, don't fix it." Marriage doesn't work that way. If you planted a seed, never watered it or gave it any attention, how much of a chance would it have of sprouting and growing?

The same is true of your marriage. If you never expand the borders of your comfort zone to include new and creative ways of communicating and bonding, what will happen to your relationship?

This may be the reason God's first statement to the new couple in Eden was to "leave father and mother." When Darlene Marie and I were first married, we lived many miles from both our parents because we were still attending school. We didn't have Mom or Dad around to ask for help or advice, so it forced us to look to each other.

We found this to be true for other couples as well.

Leon and his brother Randy had always been best friends and confided in each other about everything. After Leon married Michelle, he found it difficult not to call his brother every time he had an important decision to make. "It was a good thing we lived so far from each other," Leon said, "because it enabled me to talk things over with Michelle. These discussions brought a new sense of oneness to our relationship and helped me appreciate my wife's wisdom and insight."

THREE STEPS OUTSIDE YOUR COMFORT ZONE

In order to experience the marriage of your dreams, both you and your spouse must decide it's worth the risk to break through your comfort zone.

Sometimes, one of you will take the lead and the other may or may not follow. We would like to make a few suggestions as to how to continue experiencing the joy you were both meant to enjoy.

1. Create a safe environment in which to be vulnerable.

Since fear is a very real enemy to intimacy, help each other face it. The Bible has an interesting insight in 2 Timothy 1:7: "For God has not given us a spirit of fear, but of power and of love and of a sound mind."

Don't choose to talk about serious issues until you are sure you both are emotionally ready to do so. Nothing

destroys intimacy faster then being distracted. Decide on
a time and place in which you can both be at ease and feel
free to share. Ask permission of your spouse to talk about
a problem between you or to share a need in the form of a
request.

Never make your spouse feel threatened or rejected.
Instead, always let him or her know of your love and
commitment regardless of the things you may be sharing.
There is no need to be defensive if the other person
approaches without a weapon. Choose to speak in a
loving voice and, regardless of the outcome, smile and
hug. Remember, this dream marriage was designed to last
a lifetime. Therefore, no issue has to be resolved in five
sentences. If you think you haven't done a good job
explaining something, don't give up. Keep trying.
Wouldn't you want your spouse to put every effort into
understanding you? Therefore, put every effort into
making yourself understood.

It took Darlene Marie and me several years before we
both felt comfortable being vulnerable with each other.
She had to be sure that her feelings and thoughts would
be given genuine consideration. I wanted assurance that
no matter what I did or said, she would still respect me.
Most couples will express themselves easily when they
find their spouse is sensitive and genuinely listens. After
you succeed together in breaking through that wall of fear,
you'll never want to go back. The joys and rewards
awaiting you will far exceed your desire for the comfort
zone.

2. Overcome the routine and take on the adventure.

"How do you know you won't like it if you haven't even tried it?" asked the skydiving instructor. It makes perfect sense to go for the adventure in sports and business. What about the marriage of your dreams? Why doesn't someone encourage you to break out of your comfortable routines and do something extraordinary? When was the last time you took your spouse by the hand and said, "Let's do something new!" or "Let's go someplace else!"? It's not like you're being asked to jump from a plane.

It certainly can feel like it though. In order to attempt new and unexplored terrain in your marriage, you must choose to get out of your recliners. Doing the same thing in the same way is certainly safe and comfortable. It can also be boring and dull. What might you be missing? There's only one way to find out.

Every Friday Brice and Jeanne ate dinner in front of the television set. A few weeks ago, they decided together to join a class in ballroom dancing. "We've met so many interesting people," Jeanne said, "and we haven't laughed so hard at ourselves in years."

Attack your comfort zone with a sense of anticipation. Agree together that even if something doesn't work out the way you thought it would, you both will be the better for having tried. Don't let your fear of the unknown keep you from knowing the joy of working together as a team to improve your marriage.

Long ago, a man and his wife lived in a dark, cold cavern. They would huddle together against the chill, but they thought they were comfortable, for they had never known warmth. They were almost blind from never seeing the light, but they did not know it.

Then one day they heard a different voice that announced, "I have felt your chill and seen your darkness. I have come to help."

The cave couple peered through the darkness at the stranger who was busy stacking something. "What are you doing?" one of them asked.

"I have what you need," he said, turning to the pile at his feet and lighting it. Wood ignited, flames erupted, and light filled the cavern.

The couple turned away in fear. "Put it out!" the man cried. "It hurts our eyes."

"Light always hurts before it helps," the visitor said. "Step closer. The pain will soon pass."

"Only a fool would risk exposing his eyes to such light."

"Would you prefer the darkness?" the fire builder asked. "Would you prefer the cold? Don't consult your fears. Take a step out of your comfort zone!"

For a long time the man and his wife did not speak. They turned their backs to the light and covered their eyes.

The fire builder stood next to the fire. "It's warm here with me," he said.

"He's right," one of them said. "It is warmer."

The fire builder turned and saw a figure slowly step toward the fire.

"I can open my eyes now," the woman proclaimed. "I can see."

"Come closer," invited the fire builder.

She did and stepped into the ring of light. "It's so warm!" She extended her hands and sighed as her chill began to pass. "Come, my love. Feel the warmth."

"Silence, woman!" her mate cried. "Dare you lead us into your folly? Leave if you want to, and take your light with you."

She turned to the fire builder. "Why won't he come?"

"He chooses the cold for it's what he knows. He'd rather be cold in his comfort zone than change. Will you leave the fire now?"

She paused and then answered, "I cannot. I cannot bear the cold. But nor can I bear the thought of my husband alone in his darkness."

"You don't have to," the fire builder said, reaching into the fire and removing a stick. "Carry this to him. Show him that the light is more beautiful than the dark. Let him feel the warmth of the fire."

And so she took the small flame and stepped into the shadows.[1]

3. Pledge to be completely honest with and loyal to each other.

Any couple can appear to be happily married on the outside; it's what's happening on the *inside* that counts. If you and your spouse are surviving by keeping a polite distance from each other, take heart. New beginnings are the best kind. The sun rises every day, the flowers bloom every spring, and God's mercies are new every morning. Even if your spouse is skeptical or uncooperative, you be the one to take the first step. After all, most marriages have been saved because one of the partners made the commitment to be the one to make things work.

Nothing destroys intimacy quicker than a lack of trust. If you cannot be certain that your spouse is trustworthy with the affairs of your heart, why would you share them? Being honest and open with each other is risky. Therefore, it is critical that you choose to honor one another's feelings. Hiding your true feelings from your spouse is not only unfair to you both, but it hinders you from being able to enjoy the intimacy you both long to have in your marriage.

When honesty is the policy of your marriage, you'll find it much easier to forgive one another as well. Sometimes hurts are caused unintentionally, but only in knowing the other person's story can you accept the apology and go on. Even if your spouse doesn't ask for forgiveness, you can be honest in your response to the offense and then choose to give him or her the gift of forgiveness. Everyone makes mistakes. When you make excuses rather than admit your faults to each other, you suffer needlessly. Don't expect your spouse to be perfect, because if he was, he may not have married you!

Another key to living the marriage of your dreams is *loyalty*. Early on in our marriage, Darlene Marie and I noticed that some of our married friends seemed to take delight in making their spouse the object of a joke. It may have been a silly mistake the husband made or an unusual habit the wife had that made everyone laugh. Although their spouse laughed at the time, making a joke at their expense wasn't the loyal thing to do. We made the decision to always speak well of each other in private as well as in public. That's a decision we've never regretted.

Couples who choose to support one another also make it easier to get through the hard times. Being loyal is evidence that you love the other person more than yourself. Listen to how the Bible describes that kind of love:

> Love suffers long and is kind; love does not envy; love does not parade itself, is not puffed up; does not behave rudely, does not seek its own, is not provoked, thinks no evil; does not rejoice in iniquity, but rejoices in the truth; bears all things, believes all things, hopes all things, endures all things. Love never fails.
>
> I CORINTHIANS 13:4–8

Love and loyalty go together in the dream marriage. Find creative ways to cement your loyalty to each other. You might even come up with some ways to demonstrate your loyalty, such as greeting your wife in an affectionate way in front of your coworkers, choosing to keep a date night with your husband when your sister has tickets to your favorite play, or keeping special occasions with each other no matter what else comes up. The important thing is that by being loyal, you are watching over each other's hearts.

Our opening story about Kim and Gregg demonstrates the frustration and pain that comes when one or both partners refuse to break through their comfort zone and become transparent. Imagine what your next season of marriage will be like if you continue to encourage each other in this area. There is no limit to the territory you are yet to discover and the intimacy you are meant to enjoy. Remember that it takes courage to step out together, but you will find the results exhilarating. And you will be better prepared to help each other face what comes next in the journey toward the marriage of your dreams.

---

1. The story about "seeing the light" is a retelling of a traditional story, inspired by "The Cave" in Margaret Silk, *One Hundred Wisdom Stories from Around the World* (Oxford: Lion Publishing, 2003).

CHAPTER TEN

BORDERLAND

PRINCIPLE #3
Consider the expectations of others,
but choose your spouse

"How will the two of you survive so far away from us?" Mom asked.

"After yesterday, I wonder how they would have survived so close to us," said Dad, attempting to lighten the conversation.

"I can't believe how selfish you are," IdeaMan said. "You just want to go off on adventures, but you forget your work is here."

Back and forth they argued and sought to convince Ordinary and Wonder Molly that what they wanted to do was a complete mistake.

I can't think of anything more wonderful," said Renee at a high school retreat, "than to marry your best friend!"

Four years later, that's exactly what happened. She and Todd met during their first year of college and became close friends. By the time they graduated, their friendship had blossomed into a love relationship that led to the church altar.

Do you consider your spouse your best friend?

In our last chapter we talked about how comfort zones can keep you from discovering the intimacy you were meant to enjoy in marriage. Each time you succeed and break through a comfort zone in an area of your marriage, you bond more closely to each other. You work through feelings, beliefs, and internal barriers that threaten over time to derail your relationship. When you enter the next stage, called BorderLand, the challenges awaiting you won't come from within but from without. Therefore, it's important to be assured your spouse will choose you above everyone else.

Where do couples normally want to go on their honeymoon? As far as possible from everyone else they know! Being together is what they have looked forward to and that's why their destination is sometimes kept a secret. "The more the merrier" does not apply to them.

When Cinderella and the Prince returned from wherever their carriage took them, I'm sure the king and queen were awaiting their arrival. The conversation may have gone something like this:

KING: "Welcome home! Wait until you see your new quarters."

PRINCE: "Well, Cinderella and I were talking about that and we decided—"

QUEEN: "Oh, do come for dinner tonight and we can talk all about everything. I'm sure Cinderella can't prepare anything as tasty as our royal chef!"

PRINCE: "Mother!"

CINDERELLA: "Oh, that's all right. I'll have time tomorrow night to fix something special for my new husband."

KING: "Oh, didn't you know? There's a banquet tomorrow night, which, of course, you will be expected to attend."

And on it goes. Welcome to BorderLand, the place where family, friends, and total strangers attempt to define the marriage of your dreams. The honeymoon ends and the challenge begins to determine who will set the standards—you or them.

TO HAVE AND TO HOLD ONTO

If you're like most couples, you have expectations about what your marriage will look like. The problem begins when you let the opinions and expectations of others interfere with the picture you're attempting to paint as a couple. Even though the expectations of others aren't usually intended to harm your relationship as man and wife, they can definitely have that effect. Let's consider some of the people who reside in BorderLand.

1. *The Colorful Clan*

Every family has its share of characters, and most wedding albums contain the "one big happy family" photo. The biblical model, however, makes it obvious that the newlyweds are to begin a new and separate family unit. The extended family can be a blessing or a curse depending on how together a couple is in their relationship. If Mom is controlling and Dad is demanding, marital bliss for the new couple will take some careful and prayerful planning. Continual interference or interruptions by well-meaning family members can put undue stress on this fragile bond just forming.

Meg and Ryan were home from their honeymoon only a week when various family members began dropping by unannounced. "Although we were happy to see them," said Meg, "we found ourselves becoming agitated and even embarrassed when they showed up unexpectedly. After a few weeks, even the anticipation of an interruption made it hard to have a relaxed evening together."

2. The Compromising Coworker

When Bruce and I were first married, I worked full-time for an advertising agency. During our morning break, some of the married women would get together to see who could tell the most disparaging story about their husband. The negative comments and attitudes were not very encouraging to Kathy and me, who were both inexperienced wives. Gradually I began finding things to do in my office during break, but Kathy decided to join in the fun. Eventually the other women talked her into joining them once a week for girl's night out at singles bars. It wasn't long before Kathy and her husband began to have some serious marital problems.

The people you work with can have a negative influence on you by the way they choose to dishonor their spouse. Talking to a member of the opposite sex about any personal issues you have with your spouse is being disloyal. Over time, it will drive a wedge between you and the one you promised to love and cherish for a lifetime.

3. The Challenging Children

Who would ever believe that an innocent baby could be the means of starting a war? Parenting is one of the most difficult jobs in the world. At any stage of their development—from toddler to college student—children have the potential to cause major damage to a marriage. Couples who build their lives around their children rather than around each other are at a disadvantage when the family faces a crisis. Seeking to unite instead of divide over child rearing issues will enable you to look forward to a more rewarding empty nest.

4. The Callous Critic

One of the challenges in BorderLand is to listen to opinions and criticisms of your marriage without being controlled by them. Family members, coworkers, friends, and even mere acquaintances will view your marriage through their own set of values and standards. Sometimes their criticisms can be hurtful and unappreciated, in light of what you want your marriage to become.

When our daughter Jennifer married our son-in-law,

Dean, he was still in graduate school. They lived in a housing project with other married students. One sunny afternoon shortly after the semester started, the wives and children were spending time together outside. Around four o'clock, Jennifer looked at her watch and said, "Oh, I didn't know it was so late!"

"Late for what?" someone asked her.

"I need to get supper started so it will be ready when Dean gets home," Jennifer answered. She was unprepared for the response she received.

"Let him make his own supper!" one wife retorted.

"Why should you be his slave!" said another.

For several minutes the criticisms flowed in her direction because she wanted to have dinner prepared for her husband. Jennifer grew up in a home where her dad looked forward to coming home to a house that smelled like a good meal was awaiting him. She also made the choice that said to Dean, "I want you to know that I have anticipated your coming and I know you are hungry." Fortunately, she was only shocked and not shamed into doing things differently. She graciously received their criticism but didn't allow them to influence what she believed was an important practice for her marriage.

5. The Compatible Couple

One of the most enjoyable times in marriage is discovering another couple with kindred spirits. It's not always easy to find a couple who has similar goals and aspirations with whom you can also have a good laugh. It is special to be able to share your hearts, your joys, and your sorrows together. The relationship you and your spouse have can be enriched as you learn and grow with a couple who will challenge you and allow you to challenge them to pursue the dream marriage.

6. The Courageous Champion

Along with the challenging people who reside in BorderLand are those who can be of great assistance to your marriage. Couples who have been married for a number of years have learned some valuable lessons along the way. Those who have the courage to remain faithful and loyal during difficult times and are enjoying the marriage of their dreams have much wisdom to share. Be on the lookout for couples that you admire and who have the qualities you want to acquire as a husband and wife. They can become mentors and friends. Ask these folks for advice from time to time. Be proactive in spending time with them and welcome whatever insights you receive. Consider their counsel as a gift to be embraced and shared with others. Someday you will be in the position of being a mentor to the younger generation of married couples.

When Winston Churchill was prime minister of Great Britain, his happy marriage to Clementine was considered one of the best examples to young couples in England of what true friendship, love, and loyalty in a marriage looked like. The story is told that when they had already been married for more than thirty years, she once came to the airport to meet him after an overseas trip. Clementine was surprised to spot a junior minister and one or two younger parliamentarians in front of the flight information board. When she inquired whether they had an appointment with her husband, they somewhat embarrassedly confessed, "No, Mrs. Churchill, we've come to see how you greet one another when your husband returns from his journey."

It was also well known that when the prime minister gave a speech in the House of Commons, he would not begin until he got a smile from her where she sat in the public gallery.

Later in their lives, the Churchills once attended a banquet in his honor. He was interviewed by several young journalists, and when one of them asked, "If you could live again, Mr. Churchill, what would you want to be?" Winston replied with a twinkle in his eye, "Mrs. Churchill's next husband!"

Many of those present remembered the loving look in Clementine's elderly eyes—and that made them look critically at their own marriage relationships.

TAKING THE BAD OUT OF BORDERLAND

Trying to go past where you've been in your marriage affects not only your comfort zone but also the comfort zones of others. The minute you choose to do something different or important to you as a couple, the people in BorderLand will confront you. Envy, jealousy, or just not wanting you to disrupt their status quo will bring them forward to object. Since it is inevitable that you will face people problems as you progress through this stage, here are a few suggestions on how to stick together when other people's agendas seem to be pulling you apart.

1. Create your own family traditions.

One of the joys of being a family is coming up with your own original and creative family traditions. The Bible instructs you to honor your father and mother, but that doesn't mean that you have to do everything the way they want it done on every occasion. You can inform them of new or different ways of doing things in a loving and respectful manner.

Tom and Beth were weary every Christmas trying to keep both sets of parents happy and accommodating everyone's traditional wishes. One year they announced that their new family tradition was to have both sets of parents to their home on Christmas Eve for a special "presents night." That enabled them to spend a quiet Christmas morning at home without going from house to house with the little ones crying from exhaustion.

Birthdays and other times of celebrations need to be negotiated together as a couple, being sensitive to the feelings of others but being united on what is best for your own family.

2. Develop ways to make your marriage unique.

There will never be another marriage quite like yours. Therefore, be original and creative in your approach to your dream marriage. If a lack of finances prevents you from going out for dinner, pack a picnic supper and go to a park. Ride on swings and pick wildflowers. Tell amusing stories about your childhood to your children once a week at dinner. Write your spouse a love letter to include in his or her birthday card. Find ways to ignite a spark in your relationship by surprising one another once in a while by doing something special for them.

I will always remember the way my mother-in-law, Joan, did this on Valentine's Day for Bruce's dad. While Jim was out of his office at lunch, she would sneak in and decorate his walls and desk with hearts. When he returned and opened his door, he would find sweets and little reminders that let him know she loved him and was glad he was her valentine. Everyone in the office enjoyed the ritual and knew they loved each other.

Refuse to be like everyone else. If you put even a quarter of the time, thought, and effort into making your marriage special that you put into your latest project at home or at work, just think of the difference it would make. You will get out of your marriage only what you put into it, so be extravagant for both your sakes.

3. Protect your marriage from sexual immorality.

Remember the day you promised to love each other until death separated you? No one at that moment can conceive of being unfaithful.

Then why do so many couples end their marriage because of immoral behavior? Perhaps it's because they don't make positive choices regarding how they will behave with the opposite sex once they are married.

Bruce had a long talk about old girlfriends with our son, David, before his wedding. "Once you're married to Angie," Bruce said, "all other close relationships with every other woman need to stop." It's not easy to do that, and it may seem overly cautious to some, but competition with former boyfriends or girlfriends can affect the oneness that is necessary in marriage.

Even a family member who has been a confidant must be lovingly advised that your loyalty to your spouse comes first. Everything you can do to protect your marriage in this way is wisdom.

Sit down together and agree on what you will and will not do in order to preserve and protect your sexual relationship. Sam and Heather decided that they would never put themselves in a compromising situation with someone of the opposite sex at work. "We both have friends," said Sam, "who became sexually involved with someone outside their marriage because they didn't take any precautions." Temptations can be subtle, but they can be avoided if you stand together and set standards that help you stay true to each other.

THE BORDERLAND BONUS

When you recognize ahead of time that people outside your marriage can bring challenges and choices your way, it can be a growing experience as a couple. Every time you choose loyalty to one another you cement your relationship. Here are a few suggestions to assist you in making and keeping your spouse your best friend in the midst of BorderLand.

Schedule a Surprise

Everyone enjoys spontaneity. Take your spouse on a mystery trip that you have planned ahead of time. Call your spouse during the day and tell them one thing you love about them. Plan an unexpected date or fix your spouse's favorite meal and hide an appetizer and salad with clues next to their plate to locate them. Do something out of the ordinary that you know would please your spouse.

Rekindle the Romance

Being romantic doesn't always come naturally. It's essential to choose to be romantic in order for the feelings to follow. Light some candles, play some music, and give each other some undivided attention. Don't let too much time go by without a love note, an inexpensive gift, or an unexpected hug just to express your admiration for each other. When your spouse feels loved and wanted, they will not be as vulnerable in the face of temptation.

Circle the Calendar

Absence may make the heart grow fonder for some, but for others it makes the heart grow easily distracted. Life can become so busy that you feel like ships passing in the night. Sit down and plan time together. Nothing says "I love you and am here for you" better than letting your spouse know that you want and will plan to be there. Schedule a monthly and a weekly event.

Several months ago, Bruce and I realized that our travel schedules and ministry demands were not enabling us to spend much time together. One Saturday morning I fixed a special breakfast, took it to our bedroom, and we closed the door and engaged in a three-hour conversation. At the end of that time, we both felt refreshed and reconnected to each other. Now, whenever we are home on a Saturday, we look forward to breakfast in our bedroom and an uninterrupted few hours together. Some couples take walks or do projects together so they can talk and remain close. Time spent just with each other and sharing what's going on in your lives means more when you have made it a priority and planned for it.

FACE BORDERLAND TOGETHER

Don't underestimate the power of your friendship. When you said "I do," it was to your one and only, not to anyone else. Therefore, when it comes to BorderLand, make sure that your "I do" becomes "I will continue to choose to put you above everyone else." Discuss together who the people are in your BorderLand who have the potential to impact your marriage. The choices you make to remain each other's best friend will enable you to face the next stage in marriage with confidence and boldness.

CHAPTER ELEVEN

WASTELAND

PRINCIPLE #4

*Determine to overcome obstacles and
decide to persevere*

Several weeks into their journey, Ordinary and
Wonder Molly found themselves taking paths that
led nowhere. Time after time they had to
backtrack and start over in a different direction.
Their energy and patience were wearing thin.

One night, as they lay in each other's arms,
looking at the stars, Wonder Molly whispered,
"I hadn't anticipated the journey's being so
hard. It feels as though nothing we do goes
right and we're wasting our time day after day."

What's happening to us?" cried Stacey to her husband
Brad. "We've been married six years and suddenly
everything's falling apart!"

Brad stared at the floor, uncomfortable and unable to respond. It was true. Lately every discussion turned into a disagreement. No matter which way they turned, they seemed to run into a dead end. Stress and circumstances seemed to be tearing at their relationship. It was easier to blame each other for the negative feelings they both were experiencing.

Have you ever felt like the path to your dream marriage has led you into a wilderness? You naturally assume that after you and your spouse work your way through the inner obstacles—your Comfort Zone—and then make your way around the outer obstacles in BorderLand, the marriage of your dreams is just around the corner. Instead, to your utter dismay you encounter some of the most unexpected trials and frustrations.

It doesn't matter who you're married to or how long you've been married, every couple goes through seasons that feel like a *waste*—a waste of time, a waste of energy, and a waste of life. That's why we refer to this period of time as WasteLand. It's a season in which you appear to be making no progress and you're tempted to abandon the hope that you will ever live the marriage of your dreams. Cinderella didn't prepare you for this!

A DREAM OR A NIGHTMARE

How do you feel when you are in WasteLand? Discouraged, confused, upset, disillusioned. Nothing works right. Life loses its luster. It's a time in which you can become despondent to the point that you entertain the thought, "I may have married the wrong person." The truth is, your WasteLand experience has the potential to prove that you married the right person—if you understand it.

So many couples give up on their marriage during their journey through WasteLand because no one has told them what to expect. No one has shared that the marriage of their dreams will be made possible by what they learn in WasteLand. If your expectation of the Dream Marriage is that you will "live happily" without any trials or tests, then reality will be viewed as a nightmare. If, however, you anticipate and prepare for these inevitable desert experiences, you will be pleasantly surprised with the results.

From Obstacles to Opportunities

Early in our marriage we ran into an unexpected obstacle. You see, Darlene Marie and I were both raised in homes where we never saw our parents argue or speak unkindly to each other. We know today that their differences were aired behind closed doors after the children were in bed. However, our expectation was that a happy marriage meant there would never be any conflict. Imagine our alarm the first time we found ourselves at odds with each other. Darlene Marie cried for hours, convinced that our marriage was on the brink of disaster. It took us a while to understand that the issue was not disagreeing about something but how we handled the disagreement. We also discovered that "making up" was lots of fun!

You may be wondering what good could possibly come from the onslaught of trials and frustrations you face in marriage. Think of it as a treasure hunt. You don't expect to find valuable treasure just lying around on a street corner. The reason it's called a treasure "hunt" is because it's hidden and you must search for it. The seeking and finding excites your sense of adventure and makes you celebrate your great discovery.

The same is true for marriage. That which is easily gained can be easily taken for granted. Developing the marriage of your dreams is an ongoing adventure of seeking and finding ways, in the midst of struggle, to come out with the treasure that is hidden within both of you. View your obstacles as opportunities to learn and grow, not only as individuals but as a couple. It's important to respect and understand each other's point of view and this can happen only when you realize that you think differently about something.

No Pain, No Gain

There's no way to get around it. Times spent in WasteLand can be extremely difficult. You feel a sense of loss when you're going through the trials and tests that threaten your happiness. But consider the positive side of the experience:

- The more demanding the challenges you face together, the greater the opportunity to become the dynamic couple you were meant to be.
- The more pressure you endure together, the more peace you will eventually experience in your marriage.

✽ The greater the risks you encounter, the greater the
rewards that will emerge from having faced the
WasteLand side by side.

It took Darlene Marie and me many years before we saw
our WasteLand seasons as times of preparation. God was
seeking to prepare our marriage to last a lifetime. Most of
the time, we are interested only in being happy or content
for the moment. God knows that in order to build a solid
foundation that will weather the storms of life, we need to
be transformed from the inside out. And that's what takes
place as we journey through WasteLand. Even though every
couple's WasteLand will be unique to them, there are certain
common areas that most couples encounter.

Finances

Some couples are an easy target when it comes to
finances. Lack of money or disagreement in how to spend
money is enough to send them into opposite corners of
the boxing ring. Money is something we all need.
However, allowing the lack, abundance, or poor
management of it to damage your marriage is missing the
opportunity to help each other put into place new
strategies for future success.

Mike and Susan almost lost their home several times
because of Mike's poor money choices. Rather than
belittling Mike, Susan encouraged him to take a course
being offered at their community center. There he
learned financial principles that gave their lives more
stability. Her attitude as well as actions enabled Mike to
become a better provider.

Boredom

Wouldn't it be great if we could "log on" every morning to
the excitement, enthusiasm, and emotions we felt for each
other on our wedding day? Life gets hectic, husbands have
jobs, women have children, bodies gain weight and get
wrinkles, energy levels vary, emotions change. One day, you
wake up and don't feel like brushing your teeth before you
say good morning to each other. How many couples have
chosen to go their separate ways because they simply
became bored with each other? The truth is, they were
actually being invited to make choices that would take
their marriage to a more loving and fulfilling level.

Why do we think that meeting our spouse's sexual
needs when we have a headache is unthinkable, but
cheering for our son's ball game with a headache is simply
being a good parent? The choices we make in being
sensitive to our spouse's needs and feelings will go a long
way to pulling us out of the rut of boredom we can
sometimes fall into. Don't believe the lie that the
WasteLand of your marriage is too hard for you. It isn't. It
just takes determination and perseverance to see that the
small puzzle pieces that you place together on a daily basis
will someday reveal the lovely, completed picture of the
dream marriage you are longing for today. Be patient and
be persistent.

Differences

It's amusing to realize that opposites do attract. However,
after the wedding ceremony, the very things that you

admired about each other can become the weaknesses that irritate you. Sara, who appreciated Dave's deliberate and methodical way of reaching wise decisions, found after several years of marriage that she became frustrated when he wouldn't make up his mind right away about something she wanted to do. Fred, who was drawn to Carol's bubbly, outgoing personality, began to complain after they were married whenever she suggested they have guests over on weekends.

Times in WasteLand force us to see the importance of accepting our spouses just the way they are. We're all a work in progress and need to show kindness and consideration during times when we uncover a weakness or difference in each other. We are reminded in Ephesians 4:32 how to behave toward one another: "And be kind to one another, tenderhearted, forgiving one another, even as God in Christ forgave you."

FROM WASTELAND TO WONDERLAND

One of the treasures you'll discover as you leave the seasons of WasteLand is that you are a different couple than when you entered. You'll become aware of the growth and maturity that you both have experienced as a result of the trials and frustrations you've endured over time. Although the process is painful, the benefits are boundless. The real test is whether you will trust God with the depth and the duration of the tests needed to prepare you to live the marriage of your dreams.

Even though you know that the purpose of WasteLand is not to destroy but to direct you and your spouse into a more satisfying level of marriage, there are some practical steps you can take to help you with the journey.

Love by Choice

How many times have you heard "We don't love each other anymore"? With that said, the couple decides their marriage is beyond saving.

Reflect back to your wedding day. During the ceremony, you didn't promise to "feel loving" toward each other. You committed "to love" for a lifetime. Love is not just a feeling; it is also a choice. Understanding the difference will enable you to persevere as you pursue the marriage of your dreams. Don't be deceived into thinking your marriage must always be centered on "feelings." The Bible wouldn't command us to love if we could not choose to do it. Many times in marriage the choice to love and act in a loving way precedes the feelings of love.

It is often during the seasons in WasteLand that a couple makes the choice to love and care for one another regardless of their feelings. Then when the struggles subside, they discover to their delight that their relationship has grown deeper and their feelings follow. It is an act of selfishness to withhold love from your spouse. James 4:17 says it like this: "Therefore, to him who knows to do good and does not do it, to him it is sin."

We need to be creative in letting our spouses know through acts of kindness and consideration that we love them in action and not just in word.

Commit to Forever

One afternoon, our then six-year-old daughter Jessica sat next to me in our family room. She had just come home from school and had a sad expression on her face. When I asked her what was wrong she replied, "My best friend's daddy ran away." Then looking into my face with troubled eyes she asked, "Daddy, will you ever leave me and Mommy?" I assured our little girl that Mommy and I had made a commitment to never leave each other no matter what problems we had to face. When we finished our conversation, Jessica was relieved to know that she could feel secure because Mommy and Daddy promised to stay together for the rest of their lives.

Sometimes it's important to verbalize to each other as well as to your children that in your marriage divorce is not an option. A journalist once asked Mrs. Billy Graham if she had ever considered divorce. She replied, "Divorce, never! Murder, often!" It's normal to want to send your spouse out the door occasionally, as long as you don't put a lock on it. One of our professors in college told us, "If you never lay the first brick, there will never be a wall between you." No matter how hard or how long the difficulties, the commitment to stay together forever and always choose to love each other will enable you to move in the direction of the marriage of your dreams.

Prepare to Overcome

It has been said that you will never be an overcomer if you have nothing to overcome. Can you picture a regiment of soldiers going into battle? Imagine what would happen if they left their weapons behind or decided one morning that they didn't feel like fighting. The victory is won when people with passion have a plan and purpose to win. Are you and your spouse passionate about living the marriage of your dreams? Then decide to persevere in overcoming the opposition and experience the joy of conquest.

The most amazing thing about WasteLand is that it causes you and your spouse to look to God for the answers instead of each other. God has a bigger dream for your marriage than even you can imagine. Therefore, the troubles and trials that come can bring you together to the One who not only has the answer but who *is* the answer. Trusting God together will ensure that the difficulties in your life will never be a waste.

CHAPTER TWELVE

SANCTUARY

PRINCIPLE #5

Establish spiritual disciplines and
entrust your spouse to God.

Suddenly, Ordinary and Wonder Molly felt
surrounded by Greatness. The Dream Giver had
taken their Dream only to give it back to them
again. As they descended the mountain, their
Dream tucked securely in their hearts, the Dream
Giver spoke one last time:

"Live the marriage of your Dreams. . .the
harvest is yet to come."

The following morning, both Ordinary and
Wonder Molly knew they were ready to
continue their journey. They were different
people as a result of their time spent in
Sanctuary. They felt refreshed, rejuvenated, and
ready for the rest of their journey to the Land
of Promise.

t was Saturday afternoon. Rick sat at the kitchen table looking at the mound of corporate reports and shaking his head. He sighed and said to his wife, "Who has time for a vacation?" Nan put her arms around her husband's shoulders and lovingly responded, "You make time for the things that are important to you. Come, I've fixed lunch on the patio. Let's take a mini vacation while we eat." An hour later, Rick tackled his reports feeling more refreshed and hopeful. He and Nan had come up with a plan to take some time away in the next few weeks.

Sound familiar? How many times in your life and in your marriage have you come to the place where you feel weary, depleted, and in need of being restored? Especially if you've just been through a season in WasteLand. The challenges and struggles that you face take their toll on you physically, emotionally, and spiritually. That's why this next stage is so important.

When you ask a person to picture in his mind a place of peace, he doesn't usually place himself in the midst of a busy city or a crowded restaurant. Instead he retreats to a quiet place in nature, just as David, the shepherd boy, did in his Twenty-third Psalm:

> The LORD is my shepherd;
>> I shall not want.
> He makes me to lie down in green pastures;
>> He leads me beside the still waters.
> He restores my soul.

When was the last time you and your spouse chose to lie down in green pastures or sit together beside still waters? Sounds wonderful, doesn't it?

It sounds like a safe place, a refuge from the storms of life. A sanctuary.

That's exactly what we call this next stage in the journey. *Sanctuary*.

Somewhere along the path to the marriage of your dreams, God whispers to you individually and as a couple to come away and be refreshed.

In the original book *The Dream Giver,* Bruce says:

> Unlike the previous stages of your journey, Sanctuary is an oasis, not an obstacle. It's a pause where you're invited to meet with God to be renewed and to make decisions that will radically affect the rest of your journey.

BESIDE STILL WATERS

Bruce and I have always loved living near water. Whether it's an ocean, a lake, a river, or simply a pond, something about water is soothing and restful for our souls. Right now I'm looking at a picture on my study wall. It has two empty but inviting chairs on a flower-filled porch overlooking a gorgeous bay of deep blue water. Every time I look at it, I feel my heart being tugged to come, sit, and be still. It reminds me of the passage in John's Gospel that talks about "rivers of living water flowing from the heart" (John 7:38). Sometimes life has a way of drying up the flow when our hearts, minds, and bodies are exhausted and spent. That's why this stage is an invitation to come aside and experience a time of renewal.

THREE INVITATIONS

Actually, there are three invitations awaiting you in Sanctuary. Unlike WasteLand, where you have no choice but to face the trials and frustrations that inevitably surface in marriage, Sanctuary presents you with opportunities that are strictly optional. This usually occurs during a time when God knows you are in a position to make some extraordinary discoveries and decisions. Let's take a look at these three invitations and how they can affect the marriage of your dreams.

The First Invitation: Come to the Water

There's nothing like a little water when it comes to children having fun. Whether it's in a bucket, a water pistol, a kiddie pool, a riverbed, or an ocean, children can enjoy playing in water for hours at a time. Water is also beautiful, useful, and thirst-quenching. Is it any wonder that the Bible uses the symbol of water and describes it as living, still, deep, and mighty?

When you enter Sanctuary as a couple you are accepting the invitation to come to the water. You are encouraged to leave behind your hectic schedules and seek ways to be renewed. Planning time together that's away from familiar surroundings can often give both of you the rest you need.

When Bruce and I first moved from the United States to South Africa, we found ourselves after several weeks exhausted from all the new adjustments. We went to the coast, checked into a hotel, and ate, slept, and stared at the ocean for five days. The rest was wonderful and so needed.

Jon and Tina found their oasis close to home. "In the midst of a pressure-filled week," said Tina, "Jon and I discovered that an hour of walking hand in hand in the park near our house gave our relationship a face-lift."

Will you make the choice to enter Sanctuary together for the purpose of rest and relaxation? We live in such a fast-paced world! It's easy to think you can continue running day after day without the thought of being restored. Even a candlelight dinner in the dining room after the children are in bed can bring a sense of tranquility and the chance to reconnect emotionally.

It's imperative as well that you enter Sanctuary as an individual for periods of spiritual restoration. One of my favorite reasons for coming to Sanctuary is found in Psalm 16:11:

> You will show me the path of life;
>   In Your presence is fullness of joy;
> At Your right hand are pleasures forevermore.

Scheduling time to be in God's presence enables you to see things from His perspective. In a sense, it's as if He splashes living water over your thirsty soul and says, "Be still, and know that I am God" (Psalm 46:10). These refreshing encounters help you understand that seeking

Him is even more important than your relationship with each other and will do much to enhance the marriage of your dreams. You discover that a transformation is taking place in you even when your circumstances remain the same.

You're not changed *so* you can come into the presence of God; you're changed *because* you've come into His presence. Even when only one of you has spent time alone with God in Sanctuary, the other will benefit from the renewal that has taken place. Therefore, look for ways to encourage each other to enter Sanctuary together and separately.

The Second Invitation: Come to the Light

Light will always overpower darkness. Here's an experiment to try some evening. Turn out all the lights in your house and then have your spouse stand outside the living room window with the curtains open. Enter that room and turn the lights on. Notice that the darkness from without does not enter your living room. However, the light from within does penetrate the darkness outside and enables your spouse to see objects around him more clearly.

Whenever anything in our life is brought to the light, we feel vulnerable. Having our flaws and weaknesses exposed is both terrible and tremendous. It is terrible to recognize and admit that we are imperfect people. It's also difficult to say, "I'm sorry," and ask for forgiveness. However, as you choose to humble yourself and extend kindness and understanding to your spouse, it will be tremendous to watch your relationship go to a deeper level.

Many times during this period in Sanctuary, hurts and feelings from the past will surface and need to be shared. Ross and Janet discovered this one night when their conversation turned to the early years of their marriage. "Janet began to cry as she recalled some situations that had hurt her years earlier," Ross shared. "I had no idea that my insensitive actions had caused her such pain, and I was able to ask her forgiveness." Being open and honest with each other about hurts from the past will bring healing and new life into your relationship.

You know how awkward you feel around your spouse when things are not right between you. It's the same in your relationship with God. Only as you come to God and allow Him to cleanse and comfort you are you then ready to commune with Him more intimately. The closer you get to God, the more you will be aware of areas that need His touch. That's why we are encouraged to

> be clothed with humility, for "God resists the proud, but gives grace to the humble." Therefore humble yourselves under the mighty hand of God, that He may exalt you in due time, casting all your care upon Him, for He cares for you.
>
> I PETER 5:5−7

As the light of God's goodness penetrates the dark areas of your life, it will release you to embrace His love, forgiveness, and healing. Times of repentance before God will not only bring cleansing, but you will also come to experience His mercy and compassion. The more you commune with Him, the more prepared you will be for the final invitation.

The Third Invitation: *Come to the Summit*

Only as you gain confidence in the character of God and know that His heart extends toward you in love can you climb the summit. You might think of it as a mountaintop experience. Jared, who is a mountain climber, said, "I know people who have a passion to reach the top, who consider nothing too great a sacrifice to reach their goal."

Do you have that kind of passion when it comes to achieving the marriage of your dreams? Then you will be in for a shock when you realize what it will cost you. You already have the perfect picture in your mind of what you want your marriage to become. Words like unconditional love, harmony, fulfillment, enjoyment, and romance are all included in your description of the marriage of your dreams.

The problem comes when the person you married doesn't cooperate with you in making these words a reality. Let's face it; most couples have moments when they think they would be happier married to someone else.

The truth is, the person you married is the one you want to be happy with. Picture you and your spouse trying to scale a rock cliff, roped to each other and halfway to the top. If you don't move together, supporting each other, it could mean sure disaster. That's why this last invitation from God is so significant.

It is usually at a point of crisis that God will quietly whisper, "Surrender your dream marriage to Me." Everything in you wants to fight, hold on, and struggle to survive. However, God knows that until you are willing to let go of your idealistic picture, He cannot fashion your marriage into what it was meant to be.

Surrender is a dying process that relinquishes what you think you want in order to eventually get what you really need. Consider what Jesus said in John 12:24–25:

> "Most assuredly, I say to you, unless a grain of wheat falls into the ground and dies, it remains alone; but if it dies, it produces much grain. He who loves his life will lose it, and he who hates his life in this world will keep it for eternal life."

You may be at a place where you have given up on your marriage. Instead, give your marriage up to God and ask Him to show you how to do things His way. It may mean believing God for the impossible, but many couples have found that only after they surrendered their broken marriage was God able to put the pieces together in a way they never imagined.

The second whisper you will hear from God is, "Surrender your spouse to Me." This request has to do with expectations. It's normal to expect your spouse never to be unfaithful, never to gain fifty pounds, never to get chronically ill, or never to get old before his time. However, when you relinquish your rights to your spouse, you are trusting God to provide the grace needed for whatever circumstances you may have to face.

"It wasn't until I entrusted Jay to God," Terry said, "that I was free to enjoy him instead of always trying to change him. In releasing my husband, I discovered that it's my job to make him happy and God's job to make him holy. Once I got out of the way, God was able to bring about real life-change in both of us. Placing Jay in God's hands has brought peace and contentment that I never had before."

If your spouse were to become terminally ill, lose a job, or be disloyal to you, only your times spent in Sanctuary with God will enable you to hold fast to your commitment at the altar to love and cherish him or her for richer or for poorer, in sickness and in health.

STREAMS IN THE DESERT

As a couple, it's wonderful to establish spiritual disciplines like reading the Bible, praying together, journaling, and even fasting when you face a difficult decision. Going on a missions trip once a year or sacrificing in order to give to something God cares about can be a bonding experience. Just remember that you are responsible for your own spiritual life, not your spouse's. Therefore, whether or not they choose to join you, it's important that you respond to God's invitation to come to Him for whatever your heart needs. Accept each other where you are today and encourage your spouse by your example, trusting God to accomplish great things.

The purpose of a dream marriage is more far-reaching than just two people finding happiness. God's plan for you and your spouse is eternal. He desires to use your marriage as a picture to the world and a blessing to others. If a couple holds selfishly to their dream marriage, never entrusting it or each other to God, they will forfeit the joy of seeing God work through them to encourage others who are struggling to also make it for a lifetime.

Your time in Sanctuary promises to be rich with possibilities. It can be a time of refreshment, relinquishment, and release. It's like taking a drink of clear, cool water after coming off the burning desert. But remember, whether or not you enter Sanctuary, how deeply you respond to the three invitations, and what you take with you from Sanctuary is strictly your choice.

I hope you don't miss the incredible treasures that await you there. They will be indispensable in preparation for the next stage in the marriage of your dreams—the Valley of Giants.

CHAPTER THIRTEEN

VALLEY OF GIANTS

PRINCIPLE #6
*Face your giants and
fight them together.*

Wonder Molly spun around and Ordinary ran
into her, knocking them both to the ground.

"Well, then," she said in a frustrated tone of
voice, "come help me!"

"You don't understand. It's good to have the
courage to fight, but Giants are so large that,
alone, we are powerless against them. Don't you
remember what we learned in Sanctuary?"

Sitting by the side of the road, Ordinary
reminded Wonder Molly that the Dream Giver
promised to be with them throughout their
journey. "But He also said, 'Call to Me, and I
will answer you, and show you great and mighty
things...'"

*T*hey sat in a small circle—five women whose husbands were suffering from addictions. "I never believed when I married that I would be in this position today," one woman said. The woman to her right nodded sympathetically and added, "After twenty years of marriage, I certainly didn't expect to have to deal with these horrendous challenges facing me." "The truth is," continued the third wife, "no one prepared me for what I'm experiencing. It's like walking through a valley that continually overwhelms me."

Those are honest feelings of all who enter this next stage in marriage. It's called the Valley of Giants because what you face there are far greater challenge than what you believe you can possibly handle. These challenges are different from the trials and frustrations in WasteLand, where the refining process brings about maturity and develops you as a couple. This time, you are at war, the Giants are real, and the marriage of your dreams is at stake.

Giants take on all sorts of shapes, but their size is always large and intimidating. That's how you know you're facing a Giant. Every marriage is unique, and therefore the Giants that you and your spouse face will be unique to your lives and circumstances. Fighting a Giant requires wisdom, courage, and faith.

1. Wisdom—Everything you've learned along the way in your journey to the marriage of your dreams will be required to face your Giants. The stages you have gone through were preparation to enable you to be strong and have the discernment to know who you are fighting

against. Some couples begin to fight each other rather than the Giant who is confronting them.

"When Rod's daughter from a previous marriage moved in with us," Susan shared, "she was angry and hostile. We found ourselves suddenly divided on issues instead of uniting in order to help her with her problems. When we began to support each other, she began to change for the better."

2. Courage—When you've learned the lessons in WasteLand and have seen how God used the difficult times to strengthen and mature you as a couple, you'll be able to take courage in approaching your Giants. Waging a brave battle against your most fierce Giant will deepen your love and respect for each other and reinforce your relationship.

Michael had been unhappy in his job for years and had started a part-time landscaping business. His wife encouraged him to quit his job while she worked at a nursing home in the evenings until his business could support their family. "I love what I'm doing now and am making more money than before," Michael said. "And I couldn't have done it without the woman I was smart enough to marry."

3. Faith—Giants are intimidating and intend to tear your marriage apart. The truth is, you are weak in comparison to the Giant standing before you. Therefore, Giants cannot be taken on your own. You need faith in God.

That's why those couples who choose to accept the invitations in Sanctuary have the fortitude to fight the Giants in the Valley. They've grown in their relationship with God and each other.

Diane and Paul sat at the hospital day after day for six weeks. Their daughter had been in an accident and had slipped into a coma. The doctor said she could hear them so they talked to her, laughed, cried, and prayed for her. "Every night as we drove home," Paul recalls, "we would thank God for giving us another day with her." Diane and Paul held on to each other and their faith in God. "One night we knew it was time to give her back to God," Diane said with tears in her eyes. "And the next day she opened her eyes and came out of the coma."

WILL THE REAL GIANT PLEASE STAND UP

When we use the word *Giant* we're talking about critical challenges in life. Some of these challenges you have no control over; some are of your own making. But they are Giants because they are an overwhelming obstacle on the road to the marriage of your dreams. If not handled properly, they can be the undoing of all you've worked to achieve together. Let's take a look at some of the most common Giants:

1. *The Giant of Finances*

A financial crisis can bring tremendous pressure on a marriage relationship. In WasteLand you may have encountered financial frustrations such as not having enough savings to go on a vacation or disagreeing on how to spend your Christmas bonus. However, ongoing financial strain or continued habits that eat away at your sense of security can loom over your marriage and threaten you as a couple. "Dan can't hold a job longer than six months," his wife complained, "so how does he expect us to ever get out of debt?" Amy and Brad were always arguing over the bounced checks from her extravagant purchases. "I can't work more than two jobs," Brad said angrily. "Amy thinks money grows on trees!" Having no solution in sight is a grim and gruesome Giant.

2. The Giant of Family

The love and support of family members is a wonderful thing, yet there are times when a family member can unintentionally threaten to undo your marriage. For instance, Ray and Sandy faced a difficult decision recently when her father left her invalid mother. "Ray and I couldn't come to an understanding over what to do with my mom," Sandy said. "Ray wanted to put her in a nursing home and I wanted her to stay with us." Dealing with aging parents, the death of a family member, or problems presented by children or grandchildren can position a Giant right in front of you.

3. The Giant of Failure

Although we know there are no perfect people in this world, ourselves included, we still don't like to fail in anything we do. But there's a difference between failing and considering yourself a failure. The loss of a job or a coveted position can take its toll on your marriage. Handling your spouse's addiction so that you don't accept responsibility for his or her choices is a huge Giant for some. Roy and Deb's fourth son became a Giant in their marriage. "Bryan's rebellion made us feel like failures as parents," Roy confessed. "In our pain and shame we began blaming each other and it almost cost us our marriage." Of course the failure to be faithful is a ruthless Giant. The choice to commit adultery has been the unraveling of many dream marriages.

4. The Giant of Fear

All Giants strike fear in the heart of the bravest warriors. However, it is the Giant of fear that seeks to undermine your marriage. Darlene Marie has an engraved slate on her desk that reads, "When fear knocked at the door, faith answered and no one was there." It may be fear concerning your children, your spouse or other family members. It can involve the fear of moving to a new city or dealing with spiritual issues such as unforgiveness. "When Roger was told he had a chronic illness," admits his wife, "my fear of losing him paralyzed me so that I wasn't even able to be there for him." The Giant of fear will prevent your marriage from going forward and rob you of the joys you were meant to experience.

THE GIANT SLAYER

How many times have you pleaded with God to slay your Giant, help you run from your Giant, or make your Giant disappear? You believe that God can do the impossible, don't you? You know He has the power to do anything, so why doesn't He just eliminate your Giants? What could

God's motive be for allowing such huge obstacles to come against you?

Isn't it fascinating what God did when Gideon faced his Giant of fear, which was a massive army of Midianites and Amalekites that the Bible describes "as numerous as locusts; and their camels were without number, as the sand by the seashore in multitude" (Judges 7:12). God whittled down Gideon's army of men from thirty-two thousand to three hundred to defeat this vast enemy.

His strategy with Joshua's Giant named Jericho was to have his men walk around the city and make a lot of noise. Imagine the look on their faces when the walls fell down! I'm sure no one had that strong a voice. He used a shepherd boy to kill the Giant Goliath that grown men were afraid to face. Are you noticing a pattern here?

God tackles your Giants through your faith in Him, which sometimes requires you to do the unthinkable. When God sees a Giant coming your way, He knows that you are about to be given a great opportunity. Over and over in the Old Testament, God's finest hour was when His people gave Him all the credit for the victories in their circumstances.

God instructed Moses to go to Pharaoh and let him know that all His plagues were for the purpose "that you may know that there is none like Me in all the earth" (Exodus 9:14). That is still God's desire today. It can only happen as you come against your Giants in the power and strength of the God who dwells within. When others see you and your spouse handle your Giants in the strength of the Lord and not your strength, they will know that there is no one like God!

Joshua and Moses were willing to do what God said even though it seemed unreasonable and foolish. David came against his Giant in the name of the Lord even though his family and those watching thought him ridiculous. And Gideon followed God's instructions knowing he would never win the award for the best war strategy.

God knows that obedience to Him will bring more than just the felling of your Giant. It will bring Him great glory!

TO GOD BE THE GLORY

God receives glory when you cannot explain the positive outcome of your overwhelming obstacles apart from Him. God desires that the world know and honor Him for who He is. Giants in your life make that possible. When you begin to see your Giants not as opponents of destruction but as opportunities to demonstrate the power and faithfulness of God, you will be fulfilling your destiny.

Don't focus on the Giant, focus on God and His ability to handle your problems. Never again run from your Giants. Never again think that you can fight them on your own. Never again doubt that God can and will handle your Giants as you trust in His power and depend on His Spirit. Never again question that the reason you are facing a Giant is to give God what He desires: "For the eyes of the LORD run to and fro throughout the whole earth, to show Himself strong on behalf of those whose heart is loyal to Him" (2 Chronicles 16:9).

Can you identify one or two Giants that are blocking

you on the road to the marriage of your dreams? Let's face it, Giants can be overwhelming, but they shrink in the presence of a mighty God. However, you must put the two together to see it. If you don't bring God into the picture, your Giant will become bigger than your belief in God's ability to handle it.

One of the things that helps Darlene Marie and me when we face a Giant in our marriage is to recall past miracles God has done for us. When I was diagnosed with a three-year illness, it put tremendous strain on our lives. During days when it seemed that our Giant was winning and we felt we couldn't go on another day, we recounted God's faithful dealings with us in the past. We were comforted and encouraged that His timing was perfect and He would be faithful now as well.

If you cannot recall your own miracle stories, then turn to some in the Bible. Who has ever made the sun stand still, fed two million people in the desert, or made a donkey talk? Who can speak a word and create worlds? He is the same God today who can speak a word and give you whatever you need to stand firm in the face of your Giant.

TAKING GIANT STEPS

It's risky facing Giants, especially if one of you decides to run and it's not the Giant. There are no guarantees in marriage that you or your spouse will always choose the right path, make the right decisions, or trust God for His plan. One couple we know, after twenty-six years of marriage, found themselves in the divorce court. The husband wanted another woman, and the wife wanted God to strike him dead. You do live in a fallen world, and you and your spouse are fallen people. Therefore, here are some suggestions to help you both in the days ahead prepare for the Valley of Giants.

1. Address issues honestly.

Have you ever noticed how women have a better memory than men? I first realized this at a restaurant years ago while Darlene Marie and I were talking about the things we had done our first year of marriage. Suddenly, she burst into tears as she recalled something I had said that had continued to grieve her. Recognizing my insensitivity during that first year, I genuinely asked her forgiveness and then lovingly questioned, "Why didn't you tell me about this five years ago?"

Sometimes you may think it is better to hide your true feelings and just go on. The truth is, you will set your marriage up for failure if you don't admit to each other that you are hurt or disappointed. The Giant of bitterness or resentment will approach you and he can be defeated only as God gives you the grace to forgive.

2. Affirm one another and don't blame.

Giants have a way of making you feel inadequate. When you don't have the answers, it's easy to point the finger at your spouse. Recognize that the problem may be no one's fault and that you need each other now more than ever. Therefore, seek to find ways to say to your spouse, "I love you and need you," during this difficult time for you both.

Jacob's mother came to live with Jacob and Linda after being diagnosed with cancer. Her constant complaining and unkind treatment of Linda was a source of tension in their marriage. "It became easy for me to get angry at Jacob," Linda confided, "because of the way his mother behaved." One night Jacob explained that the cancer medication was responsible for his mother's outbursts and thanked Linda for all she was doing to enable him to spend these final months with his mom. "I prayed that day for God's grace to continue to be good to my mother-in-law," Linda said, "because she had given me my wonderful husband."

3. Alleviate the stress and strain.

Facing Giants in your marriage causes tension and increases the stress level in your home. Your mind and body were not created to live in constant stress, and so you are encouraged in Philippians 4:6 to "be anxious for nothing, but in everything by prayer and supplication, with thanksgiving, let your requests be made known to God."

Make it a habit to pray with and for one another as you face your Giants. Find ways to get away from your problems both mentally and physically. If it isn't possible to take a few days off together, find a morning or an afternoon where you can do something you both enjoy.

As you make your way through the Valley of Giants, watching God intervene on your behalf, you'll be well on your way to the Land of Promise and to living the marriage of your dreams.

THE LAND OF PROMISE

PRINCIPLE #7

*Guide the next generation and
give the legacy of your dream marriage.*

"There are many couples in this needy city who
have given up on each other," Ordinary said to
Wonder Molly.

"Can't you just imagine the difference it will
make," Wonder Molly said, "when they hear what
the Dream Giver has taught us! If we can learn to
live the marriage of our dreams, so can they."

And with that, they continued on with their
Big Plans to meet the Great Need in their Land
of Promise. Little did they know, the Harvest
was yet to come!

*E*veryone in the community knows the Thompsons.
Ted and Lois have been married for forty-six years and
are such fun to be around. It's obvious to all that they love
each other and enjoy being together. Yet you will always
find them reaching out to others, volunteering at the soup
kitchen or having several young couples over for dessert.
Who would have ever believed that their marriage was on
the verge of divorce many years ago.

"I shudder to think where Ted and I would be today
if we had continued down our self-destructive path," Lois
says. "That's why we share our story openly with couples
whenever possible. Sometimes you think you're the only
ones who struggle to make your marriage last a lifetime."

Last a lifetime? Some marriages don't last even a
decade. And many that do are desperate to know what
road to take. That's where you enter the story.

In our first chapter, we asked you to picture the
marriage of your dreams. What did you want to be true of
your relationship? Will others notice your affection for
each other or your sense of purpose and fulfillment?
Perhaps they will see your freedom to be yourselves and
your ability to be at peace even when you don't have all
the answers. As you and your spouse walk through the
stages of Comfort Zone, Borderland, WasteLand,
Sanctuary, and Valley of Giants, you'll find yourselves
eventually in the Land of Promise.

How will the Land of Promise look to you? Will you
feel like you have arrived? Yes and no. As you look back
over your shoulder, you'll see how far you've come in your
relationship as a couple. All the tears, trials, and troubles

will be worth what you have today—the marriage of your dreams. However, upon looking around in your Land of Promise, you'll discover two things are also true.

A LEARNING ADVENTURE

"We're still learning new things in our marriage after forty-five years, six children, and twenty grandchildren!" Bess said.

Your dream marriage was meant to be a lifelong learning adventure. The temptation in the Land of Promise is to think that after coming so far together, you can now sit back and rest in your previous victories. However, although some major battles have been won, many couples lose the war because they don't continue to keep a guard posted at the gate in the midnight hours.

Sara was visiting a friend one afternoon when the back door opened. The husband entered and her friend didn't even acknowledge his presence. "My mom and dad have a habit of always hugging each other hello and good-bye," she told her friend later, "even if one of them is just going out for bread and milk." One couple we know continues to write love notes to each other after fifty years of marriage. "My grandfather still surprises my grandmother with a dozen red roses on their anniversary," says Juanita, "and she still gets excited." It's the little things that you pay attention to that escalate in value as time passes. Take your spouse by the hand and determine to cross the finish line of your dream marriage together.

The second thing you'll discover in the Land of Promise is the incredible opportunity you're being given. Everywhere you look along the road that leads to the Land of Promise you will see couples who have fallen to the side, wounded and bleeding. Some look too discouraged to go on and others simply refuse to get up and try again. They've lost hope that the marriage of their dreams will ever be more than a nightmare. They need someone to encourage them to keep going in the right direction. How sad to hear couples say, "If only we had known then what we know now, we would never have divorced!"

Tim and Lori invited several couples in their neighborhood to their home for dinner. "We had no idea the amount of stress and tension that existed between some husbands and wives," Tim said. They offered to show a marriage video series one night a week for those who were interested. "After only two months," Lori said, "our group continues to grow in number and breakthroughs are occurring in marriages every week."

THE SOURCE OF LIGHT

Could it be that God wants you to experience the marriage of your dreams for more than just yourselves? Take a look at the last book of the Old Testament, where God shares His heart and desire for a couple and their marriage. It says, "He seeks godly offspring." Then listen to what follows:

> Therefore take heed to your spirit,
> And let none deal treacherously with the wife of
> his youth.
> "For the LORD God of Israel says
> That He hates divorce,

For it covers one's garment with violence,"
Says the LORD of hosts.
"Therefore take heed to your spirit,
That you do not deal treacherously."

MALACHI 2:15–16

God wants His children to be brought up in a home
where parents are loyal and loving and there's no betrayal, a
safe place where children can grow and blossom into men
and women who know and love God and who will carry on
the legacy of the dream marriage because it was modeled
before them. He wants generation after generation of godly
offspring. How, you might ask, is this possible?

As you enter the Land of Promise, you and your
spouse realize that it is by God's grace that you have
arrived. Yes, you worked hard and made right choices
together, but your faith in God enabled you to do what
would have been impossible otherwise. Think of the
lessons you've learned and how your faith has grown. For
instance, take the issue of forgiveness. When your spouse
does something to hurt you, your natural tendency is to
get angry or get even. How many marriages collapse
because the wall of offenses was too high to get over? It is
only as you depend upon God's Spirit to give you the
courage and humility to forgive and ask forgiveness that
you are set free from the bondage of bitterness.

Ann recalls a time in her marriage when she had to
apologize to her husband when she knew it wasn't her
fault. "Terry and I were angry at each other," Ann said,
"and everything in me knew he had made the mistake."
As time went on, she realized that she had to swallow her

pride and make amends regardless of who was wrong or right. "We've discovered over the years," Ann said, "that it only takes one of us to humble ourselves to bring reconciliation." The truth is, God does give grace to the humble, and both of you need much humility in order to reach your Land of Promise.

The wonderful thing about the Land of Promise is that you and your spouse are in a position to make the greatest impact of your lives. You didn't get where you are by doing everything perfectly. However, even in your mistakes, you gained wisdom and insights that are greatly needed in your spheres of influence. Consider the following three opportunities:

1. Teach and live your values before your children and grandchildren.

Children learn more from what you do than from what you say. Demonstrate your love for one another as a couple from the time they are toddlers. Children are frightened and feel insecure when they hear or see their parents argue and fight. Model for them the principles God is teaching you that make your marriage something they will long to imitate someday.

Every summer when Bruce took a three-week international ministry trip, I would drive to my parent's home with the children. Halfway through our time of separation, a lovely bouquet of flowers would arrive at the house with my name on it. "They're from Daddy!" the children would sing in unison to their grandparents. "He always sends Mommy flowers 'cause he misses her."

As teenagers move toward their own relationships, point out areas that you struggled in and how you worked through these differences. It will give them a realistic view that even the happiest of marriages have challenges from time to time. However, never confide in your children things that should be kept strictly between you as man and wife. Children were not made to carry the burdens of their parents.

What a privilege to live the marriage of your dreams before your children and grandchildren. It's especially meaningful after thirty-five years of marriage for Bruce and me to watch our grown children, David and Angie, Jennifer and Dean, pursue the marriage of their dreams for their children to observe. Even our unmarried daughter, Jessica, looks forward to the day when she will embark on the journey of her dream marriage. Third John verse 4 says it best, "I have no greater joy than to hear that my children walk in truth."

2. Contribute as a couple to the needs of others.

When you are living the marriage of your dreams, you know from experience the joy that comes from serving each other. You have laid aside your selfish desires in order to give what the other needs. As you enter the Land of Promise, both of you will see that your focus shifts once again and the question changes from "What do *we want*?" to "What does *God want*?"

This is a time in your lives when your family is grown, your work responsibilities slow down, and you have more discretionary time than ever before. What an opportunity for you as a couple to be a tremendous influence on those around you. Your talents and gifts, your personalities, your wisdom, have all been given so you can make a difference. And what a difference you will make!

Ed and Caroline both enjoy working outside. "When the opportunity came to plant Never-Ending Gardens in South Africa," Ed said, "we found ourselves on the most life-changing trip of our marriage!" Hundreds of lives were touched because of their choice to go and serve those in great need. Their marriage was enriched by the people they met and the experiences they shared.

An elderly couple was eager to continue spreading the Good News of God's grace in their golden years. But both were not strong enough to get around much and were restricted in their activities. The wife could play the piano, however, and the husband the harmonica, so they prayed about it and then put a small ad in the paper offering their services for free. When people felt sick or despondent, they could phone, and the couple would play hymns for them over the telephone. Callers started sharing their troubles and anxieties with the friendly hymn players, and their Christian compassion and wisdom as well as their heartwarming music soon made them very popular. Now their days were filled with meaning. And they were in fact spreading the Good News.

3. Mentor other couples on living the marriage of their dreams.

Who did you call when you were struggling with marriage issues? I hope you had a couple in your lives that you could share with and get good advice from. Unfortunately, we did not. Bruce and I moved to a new city and then had a new baby. We didn't know very many people, so we kept the problems we encountered to ourselves and sometimes from each other. We went through years of struggle because we didn't practice the biblical principles for marriage. Perhaps that's why we long to share with couples through our teaching and writing what God has taught us along the way. It is our prayer that God will transform your marriage, as He did ours.

Through our marital struggles God proved Himself to be the "wonderful counselor." Someone has said, "You'll never know God is all you need until He is all you have." It is during the most difficult moments that you cry out for God's wisdom, His mercy, and His amazing grace for your life. Never say, "It's too late." No matter how serious your mistakes or how challenging the problem, there's always a new beginning with God. The couple that has walked back from the brink of marital disaster can, by God's grace, encourage and point the way for others to follow.

Mentors are not afraid to share their mistakes as well as their successes. You qualify as a mentor when you can take another traveler along the road to the marriage of their dreams and help them make some progress in their journey.

MISSION IMPOSSIBLE

You may be married to someone today who has not chosen to walk with you. Perhaps your spouse even refuses to go along with the idea of a dream marriage. Be encouraged that you still can proceed down the road toward the marriage of your dreams. Sometimes one spouse has to catch up with the other somewhere along the way. As you ask God to fill the empty places in your heart, you may even attract your spouse by your attitudes and actions. Be encouraged that "love will cover a multitude of sins" (1 Peter 4:8). So continue to love and pray, trusting God to deal with issues that are beyond your control.

Even if your spouse never decides to show up in the Land of Promise, God's promise to you is "I will never leave you nor forsake you" (Hebrews 13:5). He will prove faithful even when your spouse doesn't. Eventually you will discover that the journey with God is incredible with or without your spouse. That may seem difficult to believe, but realize that your relationship with your earthly partner may last for fifty or sixty years, but your relationship with your heavenly partner will last forever. God knows your heart, and you are accountable only for your own choices, not those of your spouse.

So begin today to make choices that will affect your tomorrow. What could be more rewarding for you and your spouse than to come to a time in your future when you know it has all been worth it? Remember that nothing is impossible with God. And it has always been His desire to see you enjoying a marriage that lasts a lifetime.

May Bruce and I someday have the privilege of meeting you and hearing you share that, by God's grace, you are living the marriage of your dreams!

Are You Living Your Dream?
        Or Just Living Your Life?

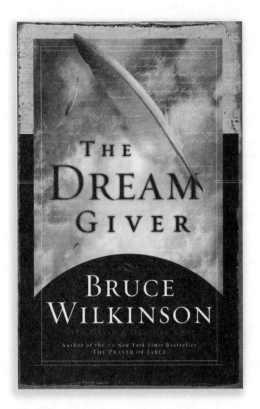

Your life dream is the key to God's greatest glory and your
greatest fulfillment. There's no limit to what He can
accomplish if you wholeheartedly pursue your created
purpose! Let Bruce Wilkinson show you how to rise above
the ordinary, conquer your fears, and overcome the
obstacles that keep you from living your Big Dream.

ISBN 1-59052-201-X
$16.99

THE DREAM GIVER SERIES

THE DREAM GIVER FOR COUPLES
Let Bruce and Darlene Marie Wilkinson take you on a journey that will give you hope as you discover the seven principles to experiencing the marriage you've always dreamed of.

ISBN 1-59052-460-8

THE DREAM GIVER FOR TEENS
It's time to begin the journey of your life. Let Bruce and Jessica Wilkinson help you find your dream and pursue it on a quest to discover the life you've always dreamed of.

ISBN 1-59052-459-4

THE DREAM GIVER FOR PARENTS
In this practical guide, Bruce and Darlene Marie share with you the seven secrets for guiding your children to discover and pursue their Dreams.

ISBN 1-59052-455-1